Children's
Services

ALA Public Library Handbook Series

Public Libraries Going Green, by Kathryn Miller

Children's Services

Partnerships for Success

Edited by **Betsy Diamant-Cohen, D.C.D.**

AMERICAN LIBRARY ASSOCIATION
CHICAGO   2010

Dr. Betsy Diamant-Cohen recalls a Rutgers library school professor lamenting the lack of professional articles written by practicing librarians and urging students to write and share experiences and practical knowledge. This encouraged Betsy to write books and articles for librarians based on her work in public and school libraries, museums, a web design firm, and a film archive. Her first article (on partnerships!) was published in 2003. A talented presenter, Betsy conducts workshops around the country, serves on Baltimore's Reach Out and Read board and on a variety of Public Library Association committees, and is currently the early childhood specialist at Baltimore's Port Discovery Museum. In addition, Betsy developed the popular Mother Goose on the Loose early literacy program, was selected as a 2004 *Library Journal* Mover and Shaker, and is a past president of the Maryland Library Association's Children's Services Division.

Library of Congress Cataloging-in-Publication Data
    Children's services : partnerships for success / edited by Betsy Diamant-Cohen.
        p. cm. — (ALA public library handbook series)
    Includes bibliographical references and index.
    ISBN 978-0-8389-1044-3 (alk. paper)
    1. Children's libraries—United States. 2. Children's libraries—Canada. 3. Library outreach programs—Case studies. 4. Libraries and schools—Case studies. 5. Libraries and community—Case studies. 6. Reading promotion—Case studies. 7. Literacy programs—Case studies. I. Diamant-Cohen, Betsy.
    Z718.2.U6C48 2010
    027.62'50973—dc22
                                                                                    2009045788

ISBN-13: 978-0-8389-1044-3

Printed in the United States of America
14 13 12 11 10   5 4 3 2 1

Book design by Casey Bayer

Contents

Part IV 🐦 Children's and Play Museums and Public Libraries

Part V 🐦 Cultural Institutions and Public Libraries

Part VI 🐦 Businesses and Public Libraries

Acknowledgments

Thank you to ALA Editions and Stephanie Zvirin for asking me to edit this book on collaborative partnerships, which proved a glorious opportunity to publicize successful public library partnerships involving children's services while connecting and reconnecting with wonderful people doing amazing things. Thank you to my public and school librarian partners in New Jersey and to the Enoch Pratt Free Library, Ellen Riordan, Selma Levi, and Dr. Carla Hayden, for providing so many exciting collaboration opportunities.

My friendship with Dina Sherman began through a shared passion for publicizing the value of museum-library partnerships. I thank all librarians and museum personnel who participated in our panel presentations at conferences held by the American Library Association, the Association for Library Service to Children, the Association of Children's Museums, the American Association of Museums, the International Federation of Library Associations and Institutions, the International Museum Theatre Alliance, the Hands On! Europe Playing to Learn Annual Conference, and the Mid-Atlantic Association of Museums.

Although I can't acknowledge each collaborative partner, every successful partnership encouraged the formation of another one; some wonderful partners have been Kit Bloom, Anne Calderón, Maureen Farley, Rosa Hernandez, Harriet Lynn, Nora Moynihan, Danielle Nekimken, Carole Schlein, Cherie Stellacio, Dorothy Valakos, Regina Wade, Cynthia Webber, and the staff at Port Discovery Children's Museum in Baltimore.

Working with every one of the contributing authors has been a pleasure; I thank all of them for sharing their experiences. Fran Glushakow-Gould has been an invaluable assistant, and I received excellent technical assistance from Susan Brandt, Celia Yitzhak, Yoella Diamant-Cohen, and Alon

Diamant-Cohen. Thank you to everyone who freely gave tips about finding good collaborative models. And thanks to Stuart, for our own special collaborative partnership.

Introduction

From the start of my library career, I have been involved in partnerships. When a child's abduction became a topic of concern in the community, my library was asked to address it in some way. I remembered seeing a puppet show on the danger of strangers at the Cambridge, Massachusetts, public library while I was still an undergraduate at college. After a phone call to the Cambridge library, a copy of the script was mailed to me. I revised the script to suit our community, and we partnered with local police to create a stranger safety program for children.

My next partnership was in Metuchen, New Jersey, where the library partnered with the public elementary schools to present a townwide poetry festival. The school media specialists and I wrote a grant that provided funding for the entire festival. The poets Eve Merriam and John Ciardi gave a public reading of their poetry in the local movie theater and at the public library. Special creative writing classes run by a local theater inspired children to write their own poetry. Teachers and school media specialists helped children choose a favorite poem and memorize it. Through schoolwide competitions, each class selected representatives to present their memorized or self-written poem. Original poems by schoolchildren were placed on display in the public library and space was reserved for the final event. As the children's librarian, I organized the event, created the fliers, sent out the press releases, provided the refreshments, and acted as the MC. It was a wonderful experience.

Coming from a large library with multiple children's librarians to a small-town library where I was the entire children's department made partnership a necessity. A group of children's librarians from central New Jersey partnered together to provide multiperson skits, puppet shows, and shadow-box theater in our various small libraries. By sharing personnel, we were able to visit schools in all of our towns and offer a scintillating skit to encourage children to join the Summer Reading Club. It certainly was more fun than visiting schools alone, and it made a greater impact on the children.

My first job with the Enoch Pratt Free Library was as manager of the Exploration Center, a public library inside of Baltimore's Port Discovery Children's Museum. Although I was an employee of the public library, my physical site was inside the museum. Because of this unique setup, groups coming to the library for preschool storytime were able to hear funny stories about body parts, to visit a museum exhibit on the body and climb through a mouth or nose, and then to return to the library for a final body-themed story and finger play. The ability to take storytime attendees into museum exhibits for free as part of each library program enabled us to enrich the typical storytime experience. Moreover, museum visitors who lived anywhere in the state of Maryland were encouraged to browse through the collection of books on topics relating to each museum exhibit, to borrow them with their library cards, and to return them to their local libraries. This enabled them to extend their museum visit beyond the physical walls of the museum. As the State Library Resource Center, Pratt both distributed and collected library books from around the state, so the museum was added to its delivery route, which made this all possible.

Because our museum-library partnership was rich with so many benefits, I was inspired to spread the word about partnerships in the hope of encouraging other libraries to try them. At an Institute of Museum and Library Services (IMLS) presentation at an American Library Association (ALA) conference, I heard Dina Sherman, who was then library director of the Brooklyn Children's Museum, speak about her partnership with the Brooklyn Museum of Art and the Brooklyn Public Library. I saw that she shared my enthusiasm for partnerships and asked whether she wanted to write an article with me. "Hand in Hand," about museum-library partnerships, was published in *Public Libraries* in 2003. We then joined forces with Carol Sandler from the Strong National Museum of Play in Rochester, New York, and gave presentations on museum-library collaborations at both library and museum conferences.

Following the closure of the Exploration Center, I became the children's programming specialist for the Enoch Pratt Free Library, and my enthusiasm for collaborative partnerships was undimmed. One phone call to the Maryland Institute College of Art led to an intern who loved creating flannelboard nursery rhyme characters for my Mother Goose on the Loose early literacy program. This expanded into a partnership with the Baltimore Museum of Art and led to another article, "Promoting Visual Literacy Using the Mother Goose on the Loose Program" (Diamant-Cohen and Valakos 2007). As the value of having an intern proved itself, an internship position within the Children's Services Department was created and later expanded to include AmeriCorps volunteers.

The Walters Art Museum is just one block away from Pratt; a meeting with the head of the museum's family education department led to many joint projects, including storytelling by librarians that complemented museum exhibits of picture-book illustration; art programs led by museum educators at Pratt; the ArtCart, a cart at Pratt displaying books relating to exhibits at the Walters; and joint design and staffing of an early childhood area that was used at events hosted by both institutions.

Pratt librarians, their family members, and some friends mainly staffed the first annual Fairy Tale Festival at Pratt. Yet the few institutions that we asked to participate responded enthusiastically, and as a result, we were able to offer multiple tables with more activities and to provide exposure to groups such as the Baltimore Science Fiction Society. Each subsequent festival added new partners, including the Maryland State Library for the Blind and Physically Handicapped, Art with a Heart, the Reginald F. Lewis Museum of Maryland African American History and Culture, the Jewish Museum of Maryland, 4-H, the Bach Society of Baltimore, the American Visionary Art Museum, the Baltimore Streetcar Museum, a local Girl Scout troop, and AmeriCorps. We also invited the Music Teachers Association of Greater Baltimore to hold its annual piano recital in our Central Hall. Children treated library visitors to live music performances, and the piano students were treated to a stunning venue with a large audience for their performance.

A phone call to a professor in the Music Education Division at the Peabody Institute of the Johns Hopkins University led to musical performances of *Zin! Zin! Zin! A Violin!* (based on the book by Lloyd Moss, Simon and Schuster, 1995) during Children's Book Week and another article in *Public Libraries* that I coauthored with Cherie Stellacio (Diamant-Cohen and Stellacio 2008). A favorite collaboration of mine was with Anne Calderón at the Maryland Committee for Children, which resulted in the creation of Buena Casa, Buena Brasa, the Spanish-language early childhood program that was a precursor to Mother Goose on the Loose en Español. While Deborah Margolis was the youth services coordinator at the Maryland State Library for the Blind and Physically Handicapped, she and I adapted Mother Goose on the Loose yet again, creating an inclusive version for children with a variety of special needs. We then brought the program to the Port Discovery Children's Museum and provided training for it at the Prince George's County Memorial Library System, which broadened the effect of our collaboration. Mother Goose on the Loose collaborations have spread even further than my local area; a collaboration among the Vigo County Public Library, Success by 6, and the United Way of the Wabash Valley resulted in a mobile Mother Goose on the Loose program in Terre Haute, Indiana. An outreach librarian with a designated Mother Goose on the Loose mobile brings the program to a number of home day cares in both Vigo County and Clay County on a regular basis.

Through all these partnerships, I have learned that often it just takes one phone call and a lunch to meet someone at another cultural institution, followed by a brainstorming session about ways to partner. Some projects are long term and require funding, a memorandum of understanding, and strict controls. Others are more flexible and incur no additional cost to either institution. I believe that partnerships are a wonderful tool for expanding resources in a time of a shrinking economy. For that reason, I was delighted to undertake this book project. By asking fellow librarians and museum staff to share their stories of successful partnerships, I hope to encourage readers to find new partnerships or extend the ones already in place.

The most logical way to find contributors for this book was to ask people with whom I had already directly collaborated and to ask others whose projects I held in high regard. The projects described by Ellen Riordan, Emily Blumenthal, Leah Wagner, Deborah Margolis, and Linda Schwartz are ones in which I have had some type of personal involvement. By traveling around the county to present Mother Goose on the Loose training workshops, I have met incredible people, such as Maureen Ambrosino, Cathy Lancaster, Shelley Quezada, Georgene DeFilippo, Margie Stern, and Elizabeth Gray, who all shared information about their exciting projects. Professional involvement with Maryland libraries, the ALA, and the Public Library Association provided opportunities to meet energetic librarians such as Dorothy Stoltz, Tess Prendergast, and Starr LaTronica. Involvement with the children's museum world resulted in connections with Carol Sandler, Jeri Robinson, and Wendy Blackwell. Word of mouth directed me to the collaborative ventures of Catherine Hakala-Ausperk and Jan Johnson. And these are just a few of the myriad wonderful examples to be found! Although there are many collaborative partnerships worthy of emulation, I believe that the ones included in this book present a well-rounded base. Together, they create a broad picture of the types of partnerships, both large and small, funded and unfunded, that other public librarians may want to try.

Librarians love to share information, and I recently discovered a helpful website on school or public library collaborative programs hosted by the Association for Library Service to Children. A number of elementary school, middle school, high school, and public librarians have shared their success stories (and cautionary tales) at the School/Public Library Cooperative Programs web page (www.ala.org/ala/mgrps/divs/alsc/initiatives/partnerships/coopacts/schoolplcoopprogs.cfm). The inclusion of information regarding funding resources and contact information for the collaboration point person makes this a very useful tool.

I would be remiss if I did not mention at this time the superb resource found at the IMLS's website (www.imls.gov). The IMLS is the primary source of federal support for the nation's 123,000 libraries and 17,500 museums. The institute's mission is to create strong libraries and museums that connect people to information and ideas. The IMLS works at the national level and in coordination with state and local organizations to sustain heritage, culture, and knowledge; to enhance learning and innovation; and to support professional development. The website describes projects that have been funded by grants and provides a brief description of what grants are available for funding. One of these grants is a national leadership grant for libraries on museum-library collaboration.

Available from IMLS are a number of publications regarding successful partnerships between institutions and organizations. In June 2009, IMLS and the Corporation for Public Broadcasting published a report titled "Partnership for a Nation of Learners: Joining Forces, Creating Value," which describes successful multi-institutional collaborative ventures among public libraries, public broadcasting agencies, and other organizations. Some of these projects involved children; one targeted obesity in children, and another addressed childhood asthma. Descriptions of twenty projects include characteristics of successful partnerships, challenges, and lessons learned. Although the report targets the projects that received IMLS funds, it is valuable for generating ideas about collaborations to consider for your library. Keep in mind that there are still great opportunities to receive funding for partnerships through IMLS. I encourage all librarians to apply for an IMLS grant. But whether or not you apply, I hope you will get lots of wonderful ideas about partnering from this book!

References

Diamant-Cohen, Betsy, and Dina Sherman. "Hand in Hand: Museums and Libraries Working Together." *Public Libraries* 42, no. 2 (2003): 102–105.

Diamant-Cohen, Betsy, and Cherie Stellacio. "Do a Duet: Partnering for Programming." *Public Libraries* 47, no. 6 (2008): 11–14.

Diamant-Cohen, Betsy, and Dorothy Valakos. "Promoting Visual Literacy through Mother Goose on the Loose." *Public Libraries* 46, no. 2 (2007): 47–54.

Institute for Museum and Library Services and the Corporation for Public Broadcasting. "Partnership for a Nation of Learners: Joining Forces, Creating Value." www.imls.gov/pdf/PNLReport.pdf.

one

Community Organizations and Public Libraries

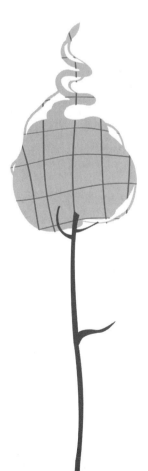

The Big Tree Library

Jan Johnson

The Big Tree Library is a summer reading collaboration between the Princeton Public Library and the Princeton Recreation Department day camp in New Jersey. The object is twofold: to enrich the camp experiences for children and to take librarians and the library outside our walls to remind children spending most of their summertime in active adventures that we are the starting and destination points for adventures of the mind, in the summer and all year round, too.

Princeton Public Library serves thirty thousand residents of both Princeton Borough and Princeton Township. The library's mission is to connect "people with ideas, information, technology, resources and each other in ways that enrich their lives and help them to realize their dreams" (www.princetonlibrary .org/about/index.html). The Princeton Recreation Department, a joint agency governed by an appointed recreation board, provides services to the Princeton community that promote fitness, wellness, and other life-quality activities. The Princeton Recreation day camp entertains more than 250 children between the ages of five and eleven for four or eight weeks using the Community Park Pool, as well as adjacent sports and nature facilities.

BACKGROUND

My daughter attended the Recreation Department's day camp when she was six years old. She loved most of it but had a limited tolerance for chaos. I asked the counselor if there was any way she could quietly sit under a tree and read for a few minutes every day when she felt overstimulated and was told no—the counselors had to have all the kids in their groups do the same things at the same times in order to keep track of them. My daughter quit camp. About that time, the board of trustees of the Princeton Public Library was looking for outreach programs in an attempt to build more community awareness of the library in preparation for a building program. Our original outreach idea was to take the Summer Reading Club to the summer day camp, complete with reading records, reporting, rewards, and actual circulation of materials. The logistics would have been too labor intensive and too costly, requiring up to eight volunteers and two librarians just to listen to 260 reading reports and to tabulate the results each week. Include the cost of duplicating supplies and the challenge of transporting all the paraphernalia from the library to the camp three times a week and it was too much. So we simplified it.

HOW THE PROGRAM WORKS

The Big Tree Library happens at the Community Park Pool, about half a mile from the library, after campers have a chance to swim and eat their lunch. We send one of our youth services librarians and (usually) two teen volunteers to read stories and to distribute paperback books at the summer day camp three times a week every week that camp is in session. The approximately 260 campers are divided into six groups: boys and girls entering first grade, boys and girls entering second grade, boys entering third and fourth grade (usually the largest group), girls entering third and fourth grade, boys entering fifth and sixth grade, and girls entering fifth and sixth grade. Each of these groups meets with a librarian once a week.

Librarian and teen volunteers arrive at approximately 1:30 p.m. to set up. They carry the plastic milk crates filled with age-appropriate paperbacks across the pool deck from the storage area to the Big Tree Library, which is a grassy area under a huge maple tree about fifty feet from the diving pool. A picnic table and benches are there to display books, and not too far away a lawn chair accommodates the reader. The children are arranged facing away from the water, and the librarian faces the pool.

At 1:45, two groups of campers, anywhere from thirty to eighty kids, arrive with as many as fifteen counselors in tow. They all stop by the picnic table to "return" the books they took home the week before. Then one group settles in on the grass surrounding the lawn chair and the other group eagerly surrounds the picnic table. The listeners hear and talk about stories for thirty minutes while the readers have thirty minutes to peruse the titles in the milk cartons to choose what they want to read on the spot and which book they want to take home. Circulation is on the honor system. At 2:15, the groups exchange places, and the former readers listen and the former listeners peruse the books. At 2:45, all campers put their books into their backpacks, gather up the towels they were sitting on, and trudge off to the camp's pickup spot for dismissal or after-camp care.

Librarians read materials from the library's collection. For librarians who spend the school year reading stories to preschoolers, the chance to share favorite fables, folktales, "fractured" fairy tales and stories with more complicated plots or sophisticated humor with the six- to eight-year-olds is a treat. But trial and error has taught us that nonfiction goes over well with the older groups. With the fifth- and sixth-grade boys, we have had great success with such titles as *Bodies from the Ice: Melting Glaciers and the Rediscovery of the Past*, by James Deem (Houghton Mifflin, 2008). Books about pets and pet care are successful, as are such titles as *My Librarian Is a Camel: How Books Are Brought to Children around the World*, by Margriet Ruurs (Boyds Mills, 2005), and *The Bone Detectives: How Forensic Anthropologists Solve Crimes and Uncover Mysteries of the Dead*, by Donna M. Jackson (Little, Brown, 1996), with photographs by Charlie Fellenbaum. For older boys especially, we have found that the more gruesome the plot or photos are, the more engrossing is the read.

If the weather is rainy, the campers spend the day inside a steamy unair-conditioned school. No one carries cartons of books through a downpour to the school, but the librarian shows up and usually reads to the double group as a whole. Sometimes this is a real challenge, particularly if the campers have spent the morning watching DVDs. On those days, we try to be extra creative,

Boys relax with a book at camp.

taking with us riddles, jokes, sing-alongs, and goofy poetry, things that beg for an active response.

What kind of books do we offer for borrowing? High-interest titles of all types, but those that tie in with summer movie releases are especially desirable, as are those with lots of recent television publicity. In 2008, paperbacks for younger audiences about the *High School Musical* movie were popular. Monsters, sports, and animals as pets are successful subjects as well. Chapter books in series such as Captain Underpants, My Weird School Daze, Judy Moody, the Time Warp Trio, and the Fairy Realm are popular—frankly, copies of Newbery Medal winners usually languish in the crates. Books are identified with a Princeton Public Library stamp and a Big Tree Library stamp. We do not bother with bar codes or any other processing.

COSTS: STAFF TIME AND BOOKS

The costs for this program include those for staff and the paperback books. We schedule an extra library staff member for Monday, Wednesday, and Friday afternoons for eight weeks from mid-June to mid-August to do the reading. A reliable and well-trained volunteer could do it, but we send a librarian because we are introducing ourselves to our new library users. We want them to find someone whom they feel they know when they come to the library.

We also have an assortment of eight hundred paperback books and donated plastic crates for storage. When we began the program in 1997, we spent approximately $1,000 on high-interest paperback books at Scholastic warehouse sales. Since then, we have replaced and updated materials at an annual cost of approximately $200 to $250, taken out of the youth services book budget. Books and crates are stored in a climate-controlled shed at the camp's site throughout the year, but about six weeks before camp begins, they are all toted back to the library for inventory and replenishing. There is no need to invest in publicity, because we are collaborating at the organizational level and our audience is essentially captive.

TRAINING AND LOGISTICS

With respect to training and logistics, we send a librarian to meet with camp counselors briefly during their orientation. It is important that the counselors know that during the reading hour they are still in charge of discipline (they know the kids' names and personalities better than the librarians do) and must remain alert and aware of the campers' behavior while the kids are attending the Big Tree Library. It is important, too, that the counselors model appropriate behavior during the reading. Big Tree Library time is not an occasion for them to take a break and chat with their peers, which would distract the children and the librarian. Usually the counselors are wonderful and as grateful for a few quiet moments as the campers are.

We contact the camp coordinator in January to get in on planning that year's program and to find out which day of the week we will meet with which age group. We also want to know whether there are any big events, such as no camp on the Fourth of July or Cardboard Canoe Day, which might supersede the program that day. For those days, we schedule a different day that week so all groups of campers have a storytime every week. We also ask whether there are any theme weeks, so we can tie our reading materials into them.

The concept is so simple, and it works so well! Do we lose books to the honor system of circulation? Yes—but not so many that we worry about it. In fact, because they bear a Princeton Public Library stamp or two, Big Tree Library books are returned to the library year-round. And while the location, near a swimming pool, might seem both distracting to the children and hazardous to the books, neither of these fears has been much realized. First, the campers have already had almost two hours of swim time, so they are saturated with pool drama and are quite willing to engage in a good book. Second, the campers may be damp when they arrive at the Big Tree Library, but they dry off quickly and the books go into backpacks or bags for transport home.

Princeton Public Library and Princeton Recreation Department have been collaborating on the Big Tree Library for eleven years. It is a winning partnership for all. The campers have an enriched quiet moment once a week, and the librarians have a captive audience for stories, word games, and plugs for library programs. Librarians love responding to the "Hi, Library Lady!" greetings shouted across the complex as we arrive on-site, and when a child asks, "Do you remember me from camp?" we always respond with a "yes!" any time during the year.

About the Author

Jan Johnson has been manager of youth services at the Princeton Public Library (NJ) since 1998, having been reference and children's librarian there for the previous nineteen years. She served on the Association for Library Services for Children's 2007 Notable Children's Videos Committee and the 2009 Randolph Caldecott Committee and has been secretary and treasurer of the Children's Services Section of the New Jersey Library Association. She strongly believes that going to where the children are is the first step toward creating library users. Jan can be reached at jjohnson@princetonlibrary.org.

Crossing Cultural Borders

Serving Immigrant Families

Dorothy Stoltz, Susan Mitchell, Elena Hartley, and Jillian Dittrich

All parents, regardless of income, education, or first language, can benefit from access to information, resources, and support about how to be their child's first teacher. Individual organizations are not always successful in helping parents to fulfill this role. How can parents become knowledgeable about appropriate stages of development and the importance of school readiness? What strategies can a community develop to help every child become ready to learn? How can families who have limited English proficiency make successful community connections? How can a community help individuals bring out their best qualities for learning, becoming self-reliant, and raising healthy children?

THE SPANISH MASS SOCIAL

As four-year-old Doris and her mother sign up for the storytime club at St. John's Spanish Mass Social, several families hover around Viviana. Viviana, fluent in Spanish, is a parent educator for the Parents as Teachers program (www.parentsasteachers.org). The families are patiently waiting to fill out an Ages and Stages child development screening (www.agesandstages.com). During Doris's screening, Doris's mother learns that her child demonstrates indicators for developmental delays. Viviana immediately refers the family for further assessments.

Most of the parents who come to the social—a monthly family event with community presentations, storytime, bookmobile service, music, and food—have very limited English proficiency and several are illiterate in Spanish. This may make some of these families vulnerable to misinformation. For example, some young mothers wondered how storytimes could be appropriate for young children. One mother said, "My baby cannot participate in storytime because she cannot read." It took Viviana fifteen minutes to explain to the mother why it is never too early to read to her daughter. Although a little hesitant, the mother was willing to participate in storytime. After the first few notes of the opening song, the mother and her baby daughter were smiling, clapping, and singing.

DRAWING ON TALENT AND RESOURCES

When Maryland's Carroll County Public Library established a goal to better reach the rapidly growing number of Spanish-speaking families in this rural-suburban community forty-five minutes from Baltimore, one name came immediately to mind: Elena Hartley. Hartley, born in Peru and fluent in Spanish, directs United Hands of Carroll County, a resource and referral nonprofit organization. In 2002, St. John's Catholic Church in Westminster, Maryland, began offering Spanish-language Mass. Churchgoers seeking advice on finding prenatal care, applying for a driver's license, and registering their children for school inundated Hartley after mass. She made it her mission to empower

Women with young children participate in Spanish-language programs.

families by cofounding United Hands and creating the Spanish Mass Social, where community organizations have the opportunity to connect with families.

The Carroll County Public Library has a long history of establishing community partnerships to better serve families. It offers six full-service branches and three bookmobiles. The library invited Hartley, the Carroll County Public Schools, Carroll Community College, and others for a two-hour workshop featuring WebJunction's Spanish-language outreach training (see the American Library Association's collaboration with WebJunction at www.webjunction.org). Through that discussion, community representatives and library staff developed a first step for improving library services for Spanish-speaking families: offering a bookmobile stop outside the hall where the social was held.

Concurrently, several agencies in Carroll County, including the library, had adopted the internationally renowned, research-based home visitation program Parents as Teachers (PAT). Parents as Teachers targets families and child-care providers with children from birth to age five by providing one-hour visits or trainings complete with information, demonstration, hands-on activities, and follow-up support in early childhood development and school readiness. Although Carroll County (population 174,000) is predominantly a white, middle-class community with top-performing schools and a library with the state's highest per capita circulation, several pockets of poverty exist throughout the area, and many children entering school score below the state average on the kindergarten assessment.

With local and state funding, twenty-seven staff members from seven agencies were trained as PAT parent educators. The educators help parents and child-care providers understand the stages of early childhood development by providing detailed information and conducting age-appropriate activities during home visits. Low scores on kindergarten school-readiness assessments and a countywide needs assessment drove this impressive community investment. The initiative was spearheaded by the Carroll County Public Schools' Judy Center Partnership, a collaborative effort among professionals offering a broad continuum of early childhood education opportunities and services to foster school readiness, and the Carroll County Local Management Board, a consortium of agencies serving families and children. After its first year, PAT helped increase scores by six points for children entering school ready to learn.

The Carroll County Public Library and Resources in Reading, a Maryland-based literacy consulting firm (www.resourcesinreading.com), developed a scientifically based research study to determine the effectiveness of the library's emergent literacy training of child-care providers. The study was inspired by the American Library Association's Every Child Ready to Read initiative and Maryland public libraries' It's Never Too Early public awareness campaign. A Library Services Technology Act grant funded the study, and the support of the Judy Center Partnership was foundational to its success. The results showed a statistically significant increase in three- and four-year-olds' listening comprehension, phonological awareness, and concepts about print (Czarnecki

2006). Several of the study's components were adapted for the Spanish-language outreach project. The library also piloted an emergent literacy peer-coaching initiative for Maryland, which resulted in an online learning portal for story-time presenters, the Emergent Literacy Peer Coaching wiki (http://wiki.carr .org/traction/post?proj=EmergentLiteracy). This online resource was used in training Spanish-speaking nonlibrarians to present storytimes embedded with early literacy tips for parents.

Another key element to the partnership has been the consistent and persis-tent efforts of library staff over the years to have a presence at the community table. Their participation in meetings, projects, and collaborations of commu-nity partners has helped librarians build important relationships and ensure the importance of literacy development across all populations.

BECOMING AN ARCHITECT FOR CHANGE

Carroll County was lucky to have several agencies come together in a dynamic process of collaboration. A state conference on cultural and linguistic compe-tence was a driving force in developing a blueprint for the Spanish-language outreach project. The project adapted several of the components that proved successful in the library's study of child-care provider training. It also adapted best practices for early learning, storytimes, and community outreach to use with families at St. John's Spanish Mass Social. A $13,000 grant provided books and school-readiness kits for the bookmobile, adult literacy instruction, and free early literacy materials for parents. The goal to sign up twenty-five families for storytime was quickly met in the first six months. The project components and best practices include the following:

> A parent survey and child assessment used as educational tools for par-ents; parents learn through the process of answering (in writing or verbally) the survey and assessment, which include questions such as "Which early literacy activities does your family conduct at home?" and "Is your child where she needs to be?"
> A take-home snapshot questionnaire for parents on their child's early literacy development (see the box in this chapter "Taking a Snapshot of Your Child's Literacy Development").
> Free early literacy materials for home use, such as books, alphabet letters, foam shapes, and puppets, which encourage parents to attend storytime, share books at home, participate in pretend play, and conduct other early literacy activities.
> Bilingual storytimes with embedded early literacy tips for parents.
> Cross-training among agencies, including storytime training for non-librarians who speak fluent Spanish.

Consistent staff participation.

The treatment of parents as partners by establishing trust and building relationships.

Taking a Snapshot of Your Child's Literacy Development

Can your child identify the front and back covers of a book?

Is your child able to point to the title of a favorite book?

Does your child understand that the print is what you are reading?

Is your child beginning to understand that print tracks from left to right and top to bottom?

Can your child guess what a book is about when you read the title and talk about the cover picture together?

Can your child guess when you stop and ask, "What do think will happen next?"

Is your child starting to connect to the story by telling you how a character or event relates to his or her own experiences?

Can your child clap syllables in two-syllable words?

Can your child recognize and identify some or all of the letters in his or her first name?

Is your child showing interest in learning how to write his or her name? (Adapted from Czarnecki 2007.)

Surveys, assessments, handouts, and other information are presented in Spanish and English. A separate component (not held during the church social) is adult literacy instruction, which offers one-on-one tutoring and group classes for basic Spanish-literacy skills for those who are unable to read or write and English-as-a-new-language instruction through the literacy council and the community college.

WHAT ARE WE LEARNING?

What are the library and its partners learning about how to effectively reach immigrant families?

Despite the time limitations of the two-hour church social, community agencies are bursting with excitement as they make strides in partnering with English-language learner (ELL) families and in connecting them to services. The community's unique collaborative staff model (Parents as Teachers training used across agencies) is proving successful for ELL families.

Despite there being an inadequate number of Spanish-speaking staff and volunteers, community partners are finding ways to consult with and coach a significant percentage of ELL families, such as by using interpreters and helping family members learn English.

Storytime presenters are trained to conduct storytimes effectively in the boisterous atmosphere of the social. Parents and children cheerfully participate.

To create a stronger linkage to library services, the library will create a Sunday storytime club game board. It will use a reward point system for participation in activities. For example, points might be awarded during each bookmobile visit when a family checks out a school readiness bag with toys or for each month that no fines or overdue fees are charged or due.

Parents' willingness to learn and grow can have a critical impact on their children.

Through word-of-mouth marketing, parents often provide the best publicity for programs such as Parents as Teachers.

Agencies must collaborate to more effectively reach immigrant families and to create positive outcomes such as school readiness. High-performing collaborations can expand the community's ability to reach into neighborhoods and homes, thereby establishing trust and building relationships. In our library and our community, we are beginning to reap the enormous benefits of stronger partnerships and empowered families.

References

Czarnecki, Elaine. *Report of the Carroll County Public Library Emergent Literacy Training Assessment Project*. Annapolis, MD: Carroll County Public Library, 2006. Available at http://library.carr.org/community/finalreport.pdf.

Czarnecki, Elaine. "Taking a Snapshot of the Children's Literacy Development," March 2007. Available at www.ala.org/ala/mgrps/divs/pla/plaevents/plaatalaannual/past/earlylittrainingsnap2.pdf.

About the Authors

Dorothy Stoltz is outreach services manager for Maryland's Carroll County Public Library. She spearheaded a successful emergent literacy training study that showed statistically significant increases in early literacy skills of children (see "Every Child Was Ready to Learn," in the May/June 2008 issue of *Public Libraries*). She oversees library programming, emergent literacy peer coaching, mobile services, and community outreach. Dorothy can be contacted at dstoltz@carr.org.

Susan Mitchell is coordinator for Maryland's Carroll County Public Schools' Judy Center Partnership. She serves as a program consultant, providing technical assistance to early childhood education programs throughout the county. She cochairs the School Readiness Team and coordinates the Parents as Teachers program.

Elena Hartley is the director and cofounder of United Hands of Carroll County, Maryland, a resource and referral agency serving immigrant families. She is a winner of Maryland's Hispanic Heritage Award and serves on several community boards that reach children and families.

Jillian Dittrich is the children's services supervisor for the Westminster Branch of Maryland's Carroll County Public Library. When she is not working, she lives in Gettysburg, Pennsylvania, with her husband, Charley; new baby daughter, Madison; and two cats, Ulysses and Shiloh.

Language Fun Storytime

Serving Children with Speech and Language Delays

Tess Prendergast and Rhea Lazar

Children with speech or language difficulties need extra support to develop the communication skills that most children learn without difficulty. For that reason, Rhea Lazar, a speech-language pathologist with Vancouver Coastal Health Authority, and Tess Prendergast, a children's librarian at Vancouver Public Library, both in Vancouver, British Columbia, teamed up to create a storytime program that meets the needs of preschoolers with speech and/or language delays. Because storytime programs are developmentally appropriate for typical children, it is no surprise that parents of developmentally delayed children find the language at library programs to be too complex and fast paced for their children, who may also be easily overwhelmed. Several parents have said that they feel conspicuous with their child whose development is different from most of the other children in attendance. Both of these factors contribute to parents' opting out of storytime, despite encouragement from speech-language pathologists and children's librarians alike.

Children who are struggling in their speech and language development need early literacy and language experiences to help boost their skill development and help them to develop positive associations with books and good attitudes about themselves as learners. In recognizing the value of early literacy in the lives of all children and in acknowledging that many existing early literacy programs are not tailored for speech- and language-delayed children, we created a unique program. Language Fun Storytime is a small-group early literacy program for children who have speech and language delays, and possibly other diagnoses. This pilot program has provided children and their parents with an opportunity to learn and practice new sounds, words, phrases, and interaction skills in a supportive environment.

THE COLLABORATION

Children's librarians and speech-language pathologists (SLPs) have complementary skills and knowledge. Children's librarians offer extensive book knowledge. They also have a large repertoire of songs and rhymes and experience in facilitating groups of children and adults in early literacy activities. They have access to storytime materials: books, felt stories, hand stamps, and so on. Librarians can connect families to other public library programs and resources, can help them get library cards, and can bring books to meet specific family's needs (e.g., autism resources or children's books in other languages).

Speech-language pathologists offer expertise and strategies for adapting typical storytime content for children with speech and language delays, both for the group as a whole and for each child's specific goals. Examples of this include slowing down; using lots of repetition; using open-ended or choice questions; using deliberately wrong or funny answers to elicit the right ones; and focusing on the types of vocabulary, concepts, and grammar with which specific children need help. An SLP can prompt children to form specific speech sounds

Brother and sister enjoy playing with felt story animals after listening to the storybook *I Heard a Little Baa*.

by using cues, for example, "make the bunny sound" to help a child make the sound for the letter *f*. An SLP can talk to parents about individual speech and language goals. Helping the children use language to interact socially with one another is also a skill that SLPs know how to encourage and facilitate in small groups of children.

THE PROCESS

We both have offered this program for a group of up to twelve children between the ages of three and five who were waiting for or receiving services from an SLP. We compiled a list of suitable book titles and selected books with high interest but low language level; with simple, linear story lines; and often with repetitive and rhythmic text, as well as clear, colorful pictures. Most of these titles were tried-and-true storytime favorites and were well known to both of us. Tess, the children's librarian, arranged to borrow or purchase enough copies of the books so that each child could take a copy home after each storytime. Rhea, the SLP, approached her colleagues across the city to recruit participants. We created a flier explaining the program to parents, but as we only had twelve spaces, we did not need to publicize too widely. Registration was by phone or e-mail. The program was free and included healthy snacks. We found a free space to use in the community, at the Kiwassa Neighbourhood House in East Vancouver. We purposely chose to hold our storytime in a neutral space, not at a library or a speech therapy office. Accompanying parents or caregivers were welcome to bring siblings along, which sometimes resulted in the participation of several extra babies and toddlers! Despite a sometimes-chaotic environment, the program was consistently upbeat and laid back, and everyone in attendance enthusiastically received the program.

We planned a basic storytime structure that revolved around one story per week, with lots of time for repetition of that story's key vocabulary and phrases during the session. Rhea prepared a handout for parents and caregivers that listed some language stimulation ideas to try at home based on the book. The handout included pictures that represented vocabulary from the story. We encouraged families to retell the story at home with these materials and to reread the book. Rhea assembled three-dimensional props (e.g., puppets, stuffed animals, plastic toys). Tess brought felt story versions of the books and foam mats for everyone to sit on. Tess also brought healthy snacks for all, as well as library card applications, library program fliers, and other resources for parents.

SAMPLE PROGRAM

Our basic format was the same from week to week, to help children feel secure and comfortable with a predictable routine:

Opening Song: We sing "Hello, Everyone," by going around the circle and singing everyone's names.

Hand Rhyme: We do the hand rhyme "Roly-Poly" to the tune of "Frère Jacques" and repeat it with up and down, in and out, slow and fast.

Book: *Clip-Clop*, by Nicola Smee (Boxer Books, 2006). The book is read slowly but with vocal expression, as well as frequent eye contact and large gestures throughout. The librarian reads the story while the SLP acts it out or uses sign language.

Felt Story: Retell *Clip-Clop* with felt animals (horse, cat, dog, pig, and duck). We retell the story using much of the same vocabulary but not word for word. We invite participation from the children as much as they are able. We ask questions about what will happen next or what the animal characters will say next.

Third Retelling of *Clip-Clop* with Toys: We offer each child a chance to be the horse and have the animals ride on his or her back, with the other children and adults contributing by delivering the animals to the child. This is great fun with lots of words and instructions and suggestions to make this a language-rich game. For example, the child might be instructed to put the dog beside the pig or to put the duck under the cat, and so on. They would also be encouraged to use those words to describe where they had put the animal.

Rhymes and Songs: Here we put in two or three action rhymes or songs that get the children involved.

Snack Rhyme: We do the active rhyme "Bananas Unite!" together. Snacks usually include two or three fruit and vegetable choices, cheese, rice crackers, animal crackers, and water. Snack time is language time, too, because we ask open-ended or choice questions and encourage the children to use language at their own level to request what they wanted for snack. We also encourage them to use words to offer snacks to the other children. We introduce concepts such as color and size by having plates of different colors and sizes to choose from. During this time, we take the opportunity to check in with caregivers and ask how the at-home activities are going. We answer their questions and give encouragement individually. Toward the end of the snack, we show the parents and caregivers the weekly handout and give them the weekly book to take home. This is also the time when parents and caregivers talk to one another. Many are isolated from parents of other children, and some have children with complex needs, such as autism. We provide a supportive atmosphere so that parents who have something in common can support one another, perhaps by going to the park and playground together or offering one another suggestions about typical parenting challenges like getting rid of pacifiers or getting ready for preschool or kindergarten. We also use this time to refer parents to other community resources and encourage them to try out a regular storytime, explaining that it would be somewhat different but that they would be welcomed there. Some of our graduates are definitely ready for regular storytime programs.

EVALUATION

We spent time after each program discussing how things went, sharing observations of different children and their caregivers, and coming up with ideas to further adapt the program as needed. We were pleasantly surprised at how long some of the children could stay engaged with up to three repeated versions of the same story, though they were told in different ways each time. We believe that this strategy met their extra language needs, as it gave them repeated chances to hear and experience the story. This method also modeled for the parents how to make stories fun and interactive at home. We also talked to the parents and caregivers individually about the children's speech-language goals. Sometimes Rhea would consult with the child's personal SLP and share information about each week's book, with the possibility of incorporating the story into the child's private sessions. When we asked whether children enjoyed reading the week's book at home with parents, many adults reported that they read the book several times a day over the week. The teachers and librarians monitored attendance and found that, even though attendance for some families was sporadic, the absences were usually because of other appointments, as several of the children received services from a variety of specialists.

At the end of each eight-week program, we asked that parents or caregivers fill out a brief questionnaire about their own and their child's responses to the program. Feedback generally has been very positive, with constructive feedback about the program start time and minor complaints about the late arrival of other attendees. We intend to continue gathering informal and formal feedback from the families and caregivers to further adapt and improve the program. We would also like to look at whether speech and/or language significantly improve for individual children over the course of an eight-week session. This would require before-and-after testing with the cooperation of the parents and each child's SLP.

Here is some of the feedback we've received so far:

> Bringing home a copy of the book to keep for the week was very welcomed, since her daughter could share the book with other family members; having a snack was a bonus, and all this for free!

This program should be everywhere in the city! (From an SLP who received this feedback from a participant's mother)

I am amazed at how much he understands the book in English after I've discussed it with him in Chinese. (The mother of a bilingual child with speech delays)

My son never shared his interest in reading before he entered the program and now I think he likes reading books that are linked to songs. (The father of a child with autism)

Parents and caregivers frequently commented on the things they liked best: repeating the story and the words several times throughout the program, facilitators' interaction with the children, using lots of concrete objects and nonverbal cues, and keeping it simple and fun with plenty of encouragement but no pressure.

FUTURE PLANS

Both of us would like to see Language Fun Storytime expand across the city. Because of the success of our pilot program, we believe that the program model is easily reproducible with other children's librarian and SLP pairs. We are currently working on a grant proposal for external start-up funding that would allow for the development of a training workshop for children's librarians and then the expansion to four or five concurrent programs in different neighborhoods.

CONCLUSION

Speech-language pathologists usually provide one-to-one therapy. Children's librarians welcome everyone to their programs regardless of ability, but as we have discovered, many speech- or language-delayed preschoolers do not attend regular storytime, as they are not able to keep up. We all know that preschoolers need social opportunities with other children their age. Children with delays in speech and language and/or in social development particularly need group experiences to build their verbal and social skills. Most children, regardless of developmental level, enjoy singing, rhyming, and stories. They all love fun! Language Fun Storytime was developed to respond to all of these things.

About the Authors

Tess Prendergast lived on three different continents before settling in British Columbia in 1990. At one time, she was considering three different careers: kindergarten teacher, speech-language pathologist, and children's librarian. She chose librarianship and has loved it ever since the first day of library school. She now works as assistant manager of children's services at Vancouver Public Library, a busy twenty-branch library system. Tess and her husband are raising two young children, and she dreams of traveling again in the not-too-distant future. She can be contacted at tess.prendergast@vpl.ca.

Born and raised in Winnipeg, **Rhea Lazar** graduated in 1986 from the University of Western Ontario with a master's degree in speech-language pathology. She has worked primarily with the preschool population in Greater Vancouver and now works in Canada's poorest neighborhood (Vancouver's Downtown Eastside). She coordinates the volunteer-run program Books for Kids, which collects and distributes new and gently used books to children who do not have books at home. Rhea has studied children's literature at the University of British Columbia and daydreams about being a children's librarian. She can be contacted at rhea.lazar@vch.ca.

Reaching Little Heights

Catherine Hakala-Ausperk

Thanks to a successful collaboration between the library and a local parenting group, kids can visit a grocery store, a restaurant, a doctor's office, and even a Laundromat while at Little Heights Family Literacy Playroom at the Cleveland Heights–University Heights Public Library in Ohio.

Back in 2002, staff from the local, nonprofit Heights Parent Center (HPC) worked with children's services librarians at Heights libraries to coauthor a successful Library Services and Technology Act grant to fund this program. With the roughly $13,000 award, the librarians went shopping! Toys and themed play areas, large and small, were purchased, delivered to the library, and assembled.

A family literacy playroom took shape that offered opportunities at each stop along the way to build early reading skills in kids. In fact, words on signs dot the landscape of Little Heights: "soap" is labeled at the Laundromat and "store" announces the marketplace. Because visitors to Little Heights are there with their parents or caregivers, the teaching, hearing, and learning of these letters and sounds becomes part of the fun together! While parents and children visit the playroom, guidelines to encourage literacy-building skills such as counting, sorting, reading, writing, listening, and speaking are part of each activity.

Designed for children through five years old, Little Heights was actually modeled after a similarly designed literacy program for preschoolers at the library in Shaker Heights, a nearby town. To start one in the Cleveland Heights–University Heights system, the HPC was a natural partner. On its website, HPC asserts, "We practice 'Family Support.' . . . Each year the Center helps more than 1,700 families play, share and learn together" (www.heights parentcenter.org/about.html). Because one of the goals of the HPC is to offer opportunities for families to interact, learn from, and support one another, the Little Heights playroom was a natural library-HPC collaboration.

Successful is an understatement in describing Little Heights today! Begun as a once-a-week activity because of the need to have HPC staff on hand to interact with the families, Little Heights has expanded to three sessions a week at the library, including evening and weekend hours. Attendance increased by more than 70 percent from 2007 to 2008, and more than 2,500 families participated in Little Heights last year. Visitors and their parents flood into the meeting room on Play Day and are swallowed up by toys in the many different play areas that are set up around the room. Although no formal storytime takes place at Little Heights, literacy is part of every moment. Children move from area to area, from the grocery store to the little library to the play washing machines to the pretend ironing board—at each stop, building reading skills. Before our recent major library renovation, Little Heights equipment was stored far away from the meeting room it used and had to be completely set up and torn down between each session. Recognizing HPC as a valuable community partner and collaborator, though, the library built a special area for Little Heights into the new design, so running the program these days is much easier!

Over the years, toys have come and gone, puzzle pieces have been loved and have gone missing, and kids have moved from their parents' laps to storytime and beyond—but they still keep coming! Library staff are used to seeing the telltale name tag taped to the backs of our Little Heights Visitors (kids are always moving *away* from you!), and if you still didn't recognize them, then the smiles on their faces would give it away!

For the library, there's been no demand for staff involvement in the popular program. We helped write the original grant, we helped purchase the equipment and store it, and we provide the space to hold the event. Fortunately for us, HPC does the rest, including staffing each session to model interactive play and offering nurturing guidance in support of their mission to promote and coordinate family support initiatives that strengthen families and build communities. In the future, we'd love to be able to offer even more sessions and, someday, work together to build and operate a dynamic, circulating library full of all kinds of toys to take home. Walt Disney once said, "Somehow I can't believe that there are any heights that can't be scaled by a man who knows the secrets of making dreams come true. This special secret, it seems to me, can be summarized in four Cs. They are curiosity, confidence, courage, and constancy." For our Little Heights program and libraries in general, there is one more C: collaboration!

About the Author

Catherine Hakala-Ausperk is deputy director of the Cleveland Heights–University Heights Public Library, in Cleveland Heights, Ohio. She has twenty-five years of public library experience and has held positions ranging from circulation to reference and management. Her book *Be a Great Boss: One Year to Success* will be published by ALA Editions in 2010, and she has presented at several Public Library Association national conferences, as well as at state and local development events around the country. Catherine is also a certified public library administrator. Contact her at causperk@heightslibrary.org.

Thrive by Five Reading Readiness Initiative

Elizabeth M. Gray and Candelaria Mendoza

Collaborative partnerships can be difficult to imagine because the possibilities are nearly endless. Sometimes, though, an opportunity falls in your lap that is too good to pass up. That is what happened in Kennewick, Washington, in 2008.

Elizabeth Gray was a newly hired youth services manager at a medium-sized library in a mostly rural area of eastern Washington, close to what is locally called the Tri-Cities. The Tri-Cities is an urban area encompassing Kennewick, Pasco, and Richland, with a population of around 150,000. Eight of eleven library branches and one bookmobile serve rural areas where farmers, farmworkers, and their families reside.

A recent survey of the Tri-Cities communities showed that less than half of the Spanish-speaking population had a library card, and many were not aware of public library services. The public library director made it a priority to reach out to Spanish-speaking families; she created a new position and hired a bilingual, bicultural outreach person, Candelaria "Candy" Mendoza. Candy immediately began to assess the best ways to reach Spanish-speaking families.

Candy and Elizabeth began to focus on serving Spanish-speaking families with young children; Candy identified the Washington State Migrant Council as a lead organization in serving low-income Spanish-speaking families. The Washington State Migrant Council is a nonprofit corporation that, through its various local centers, seeks to improve the quality of life for migrant, seasonal farmworkers and rural poor families by promoting human service opportunities. The Washington State Migrant Councils compete for funds from the Early Childhood Education Program, a state-funded, federally mandated program that provides preschool education for children between the ages of three and five. Each of the council's centers has one or two early childhood classrooms for each age, and each classroom has at least one teacher. The centers follow a curriculum involving letter recognition, preliteracy skills, socioemotional skills, and so on. The program is a half-day program on a schedule similar to that of public school kindergarten classes.

As the manager of the bookmobile, outreach, and youth services, Elizabeth was in a good position to help the bookmobile expand its services to Spanish-speaking young children, with help from Candy. The bookmobile then became a key element of this project. It was already visiting a number of child-care centers and Head Start organizations that serve low-income families. However, the relationships with those organizations were tenuous. Some teachers at the early childhood centers had a frustrating lack of interest in introducing the wonderful resources of the bookmobile to their children.

When the Migrant Council was added to the bookmobile schedule, Candy facilitated each center's application for an institutional library card. She created a system of accountability whereby each teacher at the centers read and signed an agreement explaining library services, and affirming the signers' responsibility to return the books and to use the card only for children's books, not personal use. Candy provided an incentive for each teacher to participate: everyone who signed the agreement received a nice canvas bag to hold all of their classes' library books.

Candy had recently been trained by the Washington State Library in the Every Child Ready to Read program and began presenting monthly storytimes at the Migrant Council centers. Her storytimes included both English and Spanish and modeled storytime extenders, such as songs or flannelboard activities. That summer, Candy brought to all the Migrant Council centers enough summer reading sign-up packets for each child. She also provided a special booklet of coloring pages, letter puzzles, and other activities. The bookmobile visited the Migrant Council centers throughout the summer and ushered each class through the Summer Reading Program. The results were incredible! Participation in the 2008 Summer Reading Program increased by 57 percent (273 children) from the previous summer's participation. This increase was largely attributed to the work with the Washington State Migrant Council. Of the 649 children who participated in the 2008 program, 86 percent finished the program, which means that each child completed fifteen hours of reading over the summer.

Meanwhile, Elizabeth was working hard with Benton Franklin Head Start and the Mid-Columbia Reading Foundation (MCRF) to obtain a large collaborative grant from a public-private partnership foundation called Thrive by Five. The goal was to provide public awareness through the Mid-Columbia Reading Foundation's message "Read 20 minutes a day with your child," to provide proven programs through Head Start's well-established expertise, and to provide resources through the public library to enable parents and caregivers to provide excellent early learning opportunities to their children.

Benton Franklin Head Start was the lead organization on the grant. Head Start provides comprehensive child development services for children between birth and age five, as well as to pregnant women and their families. Head Start has the overall goal of helping children from low-income families become ready to succeed at school. The second partner organization on the grant was the MCRF, which encourages parents to read early and often with their children. The library's work with the Washington State Migrant Council was brought to the grant project. During the school year, the library also worked with the Migrant Council's Early Childhood Education and Assistance Program (ECEAP), a whole-child, family-focused preschool program designed to help low-income and at-risk children and their families succeed in school and life.

The library held library-card awareness and library-card registration drives at each Head Start. They also provided workshops for parent nights at the ECEAP, where library-card registrations were available. The workshops, called Make and Takes, involved a story, a flannelboard, and a craft. Elizabeth and Candy spoke to parents briefly about library resources and the importance of reading to their children. Each child from Head Start and the Migrant Council chose a free book to take home, provided by the Reading Foundation.

An incentive package to bring low-income, Spanish-speaking families to the library and obtain library cards was developed. It included a free book for every child, a fast-track library application form, and an entry for a raffle to win a storytime tote bag. Each element was designed for the target families. The children had a choice of books in English and Spanish. The fast-track library application, in both languages, was designed for parents with limited time to fill out easily and quickly. The families could take extra forms for their family and friends. Each family or friend who signed up for a library card increased the chances of the family to win a storytime tote bag prize. The storytime tote bags were developed with help from the MCRF. The totes were full of reading readiness books and toys (reinforcing the goal of preparing young children for school).

In total, 132 people registered for library cards (83 of them to children younger than six years old) and five raffle winners (parents or primary caregivers of children between the ages of birth and five) took home storytime tote bags.

An argument often used against off-site programs is that they don't bring people to the library building, so a follow-up phone survey was conducted to determine how effective the library-card registration drive was in bringing people to the library. The results showed that, three months later, a significant number of people who had signed up for a library card during the Head Start and ECEAP presentations were likely to use their card, visit the library, or attend a library program and, therefore, gain the benefits of public library patronage.

Bookmobile circulation showed an impressive 81 percent increase in Spanish-language children's materials. Branch libraries in proximity to the

ECEAP and Head Start centers also showed an increase in circulation of Spanish-language children's materials. There was a 53 percent increase in the number of library cards registered to children between the ages of birth and five years. These results were emphasized to library administrators, illuminating the correlation between targeted outreach and increase in library use.

Because the library was already working directly with organizations that had the children and parents in-house, no additional publicity was needed. Instead, Candy and Elizabeth were invited by Head Start, ECEAP, and the Migrant Council to participate in their regularly scheduled events. Their work required only two staff people, and they used minimal equipment. They created their own materials and printed them as necessary. They developed the storytimes, craft activities, and felt boards just as they would for any off-site library storytime.

The grant provided some money, and through the grant partners, they were able to buy nice bags and things to put into the storytime tote bag prize. Overall, the cost was about $800 for prizes and in-house printing. Most libraries would be able to cover this without any changes to existing budgets.

Candelaria Mendoza presents storytime for Spanish-speaking families.

RECOMMENDATIONS

One lesson Elizabeth learned is this: take pictures! She did not get a picture of the cute tote bags! Also, she recommends making sure ahead of time that your library has a way to purchase items to give away; the use of public funds is very complicated, and you may need to have grant money to buy, create, and give away a tote bag or other prizes. Communicate your success: it is best to write up one report for the community partners and another for the library director and board of trustees. The director's report should show how the project helped achieve the library's mission and objectives. The report for community partners (whether or not grant funded) should focus on the direct benefit to the community. Elizabeth suggests making both reports user-friendly by including pictures and anecdotes along with the program description, objectives, and results.

About the Authors

Elizabeth Gray is a musician-turned-librarian and enjoys the creative spirit of public libraries. She has been youth services and outreach director for nearly three years at Mid-Columbia Libraries in eastern Washington. Elizabeth can be contacted at egray@mcl-lib.org.

Candelaria Mendoza is a businesswoman-turned-librarian. She has enjoyed working in libraries, from the library at University of Washington, Pullman, to the Mid-Columbia Libraries in eastern Washington. She is pursuing her MLIS at San Jose State University's Executive MLS program and is an ALA Spectrum Scholarship recipient. She can be contacted at nani_mendoza@hotmail.com.

two

Law Enforcement
and Public Libraries

Inviting Police to Read at Your Library

Linda Schwartz

THE WHYS

Having local police officers read to children in the library is a win-win on many levels. Community residents, the library staff, and the police share the numerous benefits.

Foremost in the list of positives is the sense of community that is created by having an officer participate on such a personal level with young children and their parents. In general, children enjoy the reading experience for the first time and most often with their primary caregivers, people they know and trust. Beyond their parents, children form positive relationships with babysitters, other family members, teachers, and librarians through the act of reading. Adding police officers to the mix broadens children's scope of community. Parents and caregivers also may see officers in a new light. The officers are responding to a situation that is neither a problem nor an emergency and get to be real live human beings, just like their audience participants. The playing field is leveled, and everyone can enjoy coming together as a community.

Storytime means a welcome reprieve for the officers participating in the library's storytime. No tickets, no uncomfortable situations, just smiles and happy faces. With more and more emphasis on community policing, officers can come to the library to lead an activity in which everyone is familiar with one another. Officers get to know local residents on a one-to-one basis. They can talk with parents in a casual setting. Shedding their tough exterior, officers get to enjoy a group experience without engaging in crowd control. They can reach into their reservoir of personal experience by using the same techniques they learned when reading to their own children. The officer becomes the cause of an activity that leaves everyone feeling relaxed and rejuvenated.

When librarians include officers in their program plans, the library staff creates an opportunity to observe how other community service professionals work with the public. The officer's style, demeanor, carriage, and attitude have the potential to elicit new and unexpected responses from the storytime participants.

THE HOW-TOS

When Police Commissioner Frederick Bealefeld addressed the librarians of the Enoch Pratt Free Library in Baltimore during the July 14, 2008, Urban Symposium, he invited them to seek out his officers to read to library users. Pratt librarians rose to the occasion by contacting their districts to seek out

Commissioner Bealefeld reads aloud to children at the Pratt library.

volunteer readers. Just as the commissioner had offered, officers were delighted by the idea. A telephone call to the community relations office of the Southern District Police Station prompted an immediate response from officers eager to read.

At the Brooklyn branch of the Pratt, the volunteer officers and the librarians planned to work with the weekly storytime schedule already in place. The target audience was three- to five-year-olds. One week prior to the officers' visit, parents were informed about the guest readers. Enthused by their new role, the officers came with the titles of books they wished to read.

Within three weeks of the commissioner's invitation, Officer Milburn was first on the scene. He arrived with an officer in training. The police department had obviously realized the potential benefits of adding the storytime program to its training curriculum. This day's participants of twenty-two caregivers and children were about to enjoy an unprecedented treat.

The visiting veteran officer selected *I Know an Old Lady Who Swallowed a Fly,* by Nadine Bernard Wescott (Little, Brown, 1980), for his reading. After being introduced by the librarian, Officer Milburn quickly jumped in and began a dialogue with the children about reading. As he began the story, his polished reading demonstrated his familiarity in interacting with young children. He knew that he should hold the book in such a way that the children could see the illustrations while he could read the text. By capturing the rhythm of the story with his voice, Officer Milburn easily garnered the rapt attention of his young audience. Most important, he knew that to keep their attention, he would have to elicit their responses throughout the story. And that is exactly what he did! After the reading the two officers chatted with the children and the adults and promised to return again as soon as possible. Parents, officers, and librarians all agreed that the program had gone quite well and warranted continuation. The librarian agreed to contact other officers, who volunteered for future dates.

Three weeks later, the community relations officer Dena Roney came to read two picture books during the storytime program. She was equally polished and captivating for her audience. After reading a picture book, she stayed to chat with children, other patrons, and staff.

The monthly District Police and Community Relations Council meeting occurred right after the officers had shared their reading talents with the library users. Here was the perfect setting to reinforce how much the staff appreciated the visits by the officers and to convince other officers that Commissioner Bealefeld had come up with the ideal way for librarians and police officers to promote themselves and one another by partnering in an existing library program.

At the meeting, which more than one hundred community residents regularly attend, the library branch manager presented each officer with a library T-shirt and described to the audience what the officer had done. Again, the officers benefited from positive attention, and the library staff was able to provide the program without any expense. Naturally, the officers drew plenty of applause and praise. Other officers, too, wanted to know how they could participate.

On June 25, 2009, Officer Dena Roney returned for preschool storytime with Officer Timika Tates. First Officer Tates read two picture books. Then she identified all of the equipment that her colleague carried on her belt as Officer Roney modeled. The children had lots of questions and seemed genuinely intrigued.

After their time with the children, the officers agreed to answer a few questions from the library staff. Officer Tates said that she believes that "community policing is important, and volunteering in neighborhoods is important for the children." She also added, "After reading I felt like I wanted to share some additional information as the kids were a great audience and had several questions about being a police officer."

Officer Roney commented, "After reading to the children I felt that some of the children who, at first, were afraid of police seemed to be a lot more comfortable and realized that police were not bad people." When asked whether she would encourage her colleagues to participate, she responded by saying, "I would recommend this program to my fellow officers because it's a wonderful opportunity to build relationships with children in the community."

A library staff would be hard pressed to create a program with better outcomes and less stress. Back at the Urban Symposium, Commissioner Bealefeld knew he had latched on to good idea, but between his staff and the librarians, a good idea became a great one!

About the Author

Linda M. Schwartz has worked for the Enoch Pratt Free Library for thirty years. She has held positions in public relations, children's services, and neighborhood services. She is currently the manager of the Brooklyn branch. She received her MLS from the University of Maryland in 1986. Linda can be contacted at schwartl@prattlibrary.org.

Children of Incarcerated Parents

Public Libraries Reaching Out

Shelley Quezada

According to a recent study published by the Morehouse School of Medicine, approximately 1.7 million children across the country reside with grandparents or other relatives or are in foster care because their parent is incarcerated. These children suffer a sense of shame, frequently have lost financial support, and often experience frayed ties with their incarcerated parent. Many are at risk of abuse and neglect. Often these children live as many as one hundred miles away from the prison or jail, which makes family visits difficult and infrequent. In many cases because of federal laws, a parent who has a child in foster care for more than two years may suffer loss of parental rights. In addition, there is a disproportionate impact on families of color. African American children are nine times more likely to have a parent in prison than are Caucasian children; Latino children are three times more likely.

Many communities have a county jail or house of correction, local prison, or juvenile detention facility within their geographic service area. In an effort to address the needs of children with an incarcerated parent, a number of public libraries have worked in collaboration with local correctional institutions to provide support for both the parents and their children who make up this fragile population. In each case, the approach may be somewhat different, but there is always a recognition that services provided by the library need to extend beyond the four walls of the physical building.

ALAMEDA COUNTY PUBLIC LIBRARY

At the Alameda County Library in California, Lisa Harris (lisa.harris@aclibrary .org) created a program called Start with a Story, which serves two local jails. The program provides for a cadre of trained volunteers who serve between 150 and 200 enthusiastic children per weekend in each facility. Harris's program is run through extension services as part of the Alameda County literacy program, which is based in the public library. She feels strongly that correctional facilities are a place where the library should be extending its services. As she says, "Most inmates in jail are going to cycle out." Perhaps as many as 95 percent will eventually return to the community. Research shows that frequent and regular family visitation can greatly reduce the trauma that children experience as a result of separation from a parent. It may also help improve the parent's chances for successful parole after release from prison, thus reducing recidivism.

Harris began working with the Santa Rita Jail in Alameda County and has expanded services to the Glenn Dyer Jail facility in downtown Oakland. The goal is to read to every child who comes in for a visit. The program features brand-new books, both paperbacks and hardbacks, which are purchased through ongoing grants. Harris aims to provide a range of age-appropriate books. Originally, she felt that the library's literacy program was serving only 10 percent of its potential population, and she decided that some of the children's materials could be better directed elsewhere. She has trained volunteers in techniques of how to read to children and has given them information about how to suggest (and give) a book to a child. The children range from preschoolers to older teens. Volunteers often are older adults, but also among them are middle and high school kids, including Harris's own daughter, who reads to children at least once a month. Inside each gift book is the label "This book is a gift from the Alameda Library Literacy Project." The library also provides information about the Bay Area literacy program to caregivers.

The program won the 2008 California Counties Innovation Award, and Harris is poised to launch it at the Tri-Homeless Coalition in Fremont, California. Harris, who is one of *Library Journal*'s 2009 Mover and Shakers, says that Start with a Story has now become a "de facto children's library branch" at the two local jails.

MARIN COUNTY FREE LIBRARY AND SAN RAFAEL PUBLIC LIBRARY

Jane Curtis (jcurtis@marinliteracy.org) is coordinator of inmate literacy services for the Marin Literacy Program in California, which is in partnership with the Marin County Free Library and the San Rafael Public Library. In 1993, she developed the *FATHERS Program Guide*, a family literacy and parenting curriculum aimed at incarcerated fathers. The acronym *FATHERS* stands for Fathers as Teachers: Helping, Encouraging, Reading, and Supporting. The program was piloted at San Quentin State Prison. The curriculum, which takes fifteen hours to complete, is based on children's picture books that address many parenting issues and models reading-aloud practice. It is designed to intervene in the cycle of low literacy seen in families of incarcerated individuals. It consists of three components: classroom instruction for fathers, gift books for the children in the lives of the fathers in the class, and monthly storytimes for children during visitation.

After successful completion of the program, inmates may select a gift book, provided by Inmate Literacy Services, for each child. Each book is mailed to the child. Storytimes are conducted in the prison visiting room, and a collection of children's books are maintained there. In San Quentin, the program reaches approximately thirty-five inmates per quarter, of whom perhaps two out of every three are able to finish the program.

Although it is difficult to track instructional hours and to define and measure success, Curtis notes, "We have men taking the course repeatedly and find they have now built a community within the prison in which they support each other as dads." In addition to the FATHERS program, the Marin Literacy Program sponsors an inmate-tutoring program in which inmates are trained and supported in tutoring techniques to serve as peer tutors.

In 1998, the program was expanded to include women and men serving time in the Marin County Jail. The MOTHERS program (Mothers, and Our Teachers: Helping, Encouraging, Reading, Supporting) follows a similar curriculum to the FATHERS program but features girls as central characters in the books used during instruction. In addition, the jail allows inmate mothers and fathers to read aloud on audiotape the gift books selected for their children that are included in the book mailing. At the jail, the classes run about an hour and fifteen minutes (in contrast with prison, where they run about two hours) and are conducted by the prison teacher, who is paid by Inmate Literacy Services. In both places, each lesson is shaped around a picture book, and books become the catalyst for discussion. The teacher promotes the idea that the books at the public library are free, thus encouraging use of the library when the attendees return to the community. At the jail, approximately fifteen women and twenty-five men participate every quarter, but because of higher turnover in prison, the numbers of those who complete the program are becoming lower.

Curtis comments that the men are actually more engaged with the family literacy program than are the women, who frequently have different issues: "[The women] tend to be more depressed and have lower literacy skills, but we tell them to take advantage of the public library because it's the last best deal around."

Originally begun with an outside grant, the Marin County Sheriff's Department now pays for the jail program, and San Quentin's services are supported solely with outside funding.

The FATHERS and MOTHERS programs have been replicated in other communities across the country. To order a copy of the *FATHERS Program Guide* contact the California State Library Foundation (www.cslfdn.org).

HENNEPIN COUNTY LIBRARY

The Hennepin County Library (HCL), in Minnetonka, Minnesota, developed Read to Me, a collaborative family literacy project between HCL and Hennepin County Adult Corrections Facility (ACF). Daniel Marcou, the corrections librarian for HCL (dmarcou@hclib.org), directs a program that works with library staff and community volunteers to teach residents at the institution about the importance of reading to their children.

Both men and women in the ACF participate in this program. Many inmates have low levels of literacy and are unaware of the critical importance of reading to children beginning at the earliest age. Moreover, residents lack knowledge about age-appropriate books and the developmental stages of their children. Not surprisingly, many have no recollection of being read to as children. A child with an incarcerated parent goes through many stages of loss and grief, and the inmate parent frequently feels powerless about how to help the child. The Read to Me program uses children's books to form a bridge between the child and the incarcerated parent. The program began in 1996, when the ACF extended an invitation to HCL to provide adult reading material for residents as well as children's books for use in the visiting area during parent visits. According to Marcou, "The program expanded into an intensive twelve-month series of classes focusing on the pleasure and importance of reading with young children."

The Read to Me program offers three sixty-minute sessions in both the men's and the women's sections over a period of weeks. Each series runs monthly in each section. Upon completion of the course, the participant receives a certificate of accomplishment. As part of the program, the parent creates a CD of the story to accompany the book. Then both are given to the child.

Marcou notes, "This is a successful program! Every year, seventy sessions are provided to teach residents new ways for improving their lives and the lives of their children. The program is measured through evaluations completed by residents; numbers of residents served (at least 80 annually); numbers of children who received books (at least 120 annually); numbers of books mailed (at least 120 annually); numbers of children who used books when visiting resident parents in jail; and by reports from volunteers."

The Library Foundation of Hennepin County provides funding for the program, which also receives grants from outside funders such as Target. The ACF provides funding to cover the cost of mailing and purchasing CDs and mailing supplies.

The Read to Me program received the National Association of Counties Achievement Award in 1999 and the American Library Association's Marshall Cavendish Excellence in Library Programming Award in 2005. Marcou also was one of *Library Journal's* 2009 Mover and Shakers, an award that recognizes innovative library practices. He is in the process of further improving the Read to Me curriculum.

MULTNOMAH COUNTY PUBLIC LIBRARY

Carol Cook (carolc@multcolib.org) is the library jails coordinator of Oregon's Multnomah County Public Library. As part of the library's outreach mission to provide services to incarcerated people, the library has developed a program called Books without Barriers, which is part of a five-week parenting class. The program consists of three sessions on early literacy development for inmate parents. In the sessions, participants learn about brain development, the importance of early literacy, and how to choose and present books that are appropriate to the ages of their children. As part of the program, Cook creates a DVD of the parent reading a book, and the book and DVD are sent to the child. An average of five to ten inmates meet twice weekly over the five weeks, and participants must complete the parenting class to get the DVD and book sent out to their children. In addition to the book and DVD, Cook also includes a Polaroid picture, perhaps with a note on the back, of the parent holding the book. Also included is a copy of the library's newspaper, an events calendar, a map of library locations, and the sticker "I Was Read to Today."

The library provides children's books in the waiting area stamped "Multnomah County Library." Visitation is done behind glass, and there is no contact between the inmate and child, so the DVD of the parent reading a story becomes especially meaningful.

As was noted in the program in California, Cook says that working with women is harder than with men. "Women are more disruptive, distractible and demanding. Typically their crimes involve drug use, which impacts their behavior in a classroom setting, while the men, in general, are more receptive and curious."

At the end of the last session, participants are asked to fill out an evaluation form. Working with corrections entails multiple levels of bureaucracy, which presents hurdles to the smooth running of any program. One challenge relates to the paperwork involved in getting clearance to send out the materials. Sometimes they need to be sent to caseworkers, who then deliver the book and DVD to the child.

However, with respect to the last analysis, Cook says, "This program has always been a very popular program in the jail. It is the carrot at the end of the stick for inmates who have to complete a court mandated parenting program."

SUFFOLK COUNTY HOUSE OF CORRECTION AND THE BOSTON PUBLIC LIBRARY

Diana Barbero, a teacher in the Suffolk County House of Correction in Boston, has conducted the Fathers' Read Aloud program for more than fourteen years. The Fathers' Read Aloud program is incorporated into the parenting class that she teaches. Barbero reaches a revolving group of students who choose an age-appropriate book for their children from a collection of new and gently used donated materials. At the conclusion of the series of lessons, the father records a tape of the story. The book and tape are mailed to the family; thus, each inmate father is encouraged to keep up the connection with his child. Barbero says that many children actually fall asleep with a copy of the book that accompanies the cassette. "This program has shown to be successful in sustaining a relationship between father and child. In some cases," says Barbero, "relationships are rekindled after a long absence."

Barbero uses such staples of children's literature as Margaret Wise Brown's *Good Night Moon* or Shel Silverstein's *The Giving Tree* for older readers. Barbero not only introduces quality children's books to the inmates but also uses the books to teach a feeling of nurturing by offering a gentle message and a sense of safety. Barbero says, "When I read them a book like *Daddy, Daddy, Be There*, by Candy Dawson Boyd [Philomel 1995], it makes me want to cry." She notes that using children's books allows the fathers to grieve for the absence of their own fathers and their own absence in their children's lives while communicating a message that they should be there for their children.

Barbero also provides her students with stationery to write letters to their children on whatever topic is of interest to them. She says that this is an important part of the process. She feels her overall mission is to allow fathers to reestablish a relationship with their children and to sustain it. One inmate wrote to Barbero, "My kids really enjoyed the books, as well as hearing me read them. Some of the books open doors on subjects like growing up without the father being present, to gangs, about trips around the world, as well as believing you can do and become anything you desire."

As part of the series of lessons that cover a semester, the prison has worked with JoAnn Butler (jbutler@bpl.org) from the Dudley Literacy Center at the Boston Public Library (BPL). JoAnn is invited in as a guest speaker who relates her experiences as children's and youth services librarian. She is there to affirm the benefits of reading aloud and the role of the parent as the child's first and most important teacher. Although the BPL did not initiate the collaboration, Butler is committed to being part of the program each time Barbero offers a new training session.

Public libraries that work in collaboration with correctional facilities to provide family literacy programs are helping to address two critical societal challenges. First, such programs acknowledge the often strained and difficult relationship among family members when a parent is in prison. Second, the program works to break the intergenerational cycle of low literacy in both parent and child. When a parent is incarcerated, all members of the family suffer. And when that person reenters society, the whole family must readjust to a new structure. By reinforcing the literacy skills of reentering inmates through parenting programs, book ownership, and support for reading, the public library is carrying out a critical part of its mission to reach out to all members of the community.

About the Author

Shelley Quezada has been the consultant on library services to the unserved for the Massachusetts Board of Library Commissioners for twenty-five years. She coordinates and develops library-based literacy and programs for English language learners in Massachusetts libraries, promotes outreach to special needs populations, and has been liaison to the Massachusetts Department of Correction. For twenty-two years, she has taught at Simmons College, Graduate School of Library and Information Science, where today she teaches the courses Children's Literature and Library Services to Underserved Populations: Issues and Responses. Shelley can be contacted at shelley.quezada@state.ma.us.

three

Academic Institutions and Public Libraries

ReadsinMA.org
Statewide Summer Reading Program Goes Online

Maureen Ambrosino

Massachusetts has six multitype regional library systems that provide consulting, databases, delivery of library books and other materials, and continuing education to member library staff. Each region has a youth consultant dedicated to working with children's, young adult, and school librarians. One of the youth consultant's important tasks is managing the Statewide Summer Reading Program with input from librarians. This includes selecting a theme, creating or acquiring artwork, negotiating with vendors for paper products and pricing for incentives, and doing training sessions on ReadsinMA. The Massachusetts Regional Library Systems, the Massachusetts Board of Library Commissioners, and local libraries fund the Statewide Summer Reading Program.

Early in 2006, the six regional youth consultants in Massachusetts began discussing ways they could use the Statewide Summer Reading Program to reach out to children and families who couldn't physically visit their local libraries. Anecdotal evidence showed that there were many families in rural areas who either didn't have a public library in their town or lived too far from a library to be able to easily visit when it was open. Working parents seemed to have little time to bring their children to the library, and other people just didn't know about the summer reading programs that were offered in their cities.

The solution seemed to be some type of online reading program. Because more and more younger parents "live" online and children are growing up in a virtual age, an online program made sense. The youth consultants wanted something that could be implemented easily in libraries of all sizes, from the smallest one-person library to large urban systems with multiple branches. The group investigated the options for a vendor-provided online registration and tracking system, and it ultimately partnered with Evanced Solutions in Indiana, using its Summer Reader program, in early 2007.

The ReadsinMA program allows patrons to register for reading programs online. Participants can log their reading through an online reading log, and some libraries include an optional review feature that lets patrons write reviews of the books they read. Other patrons who visit the library's reading program page can read the reviews and request books of interest from the library's online catalog. Each library determines its own prizes for the reading programs; the program also notifies patrons when they are eligible to pick up prizes from the library, which brings them into the actual library building. The program itself is entirely web-based, so patrons can log their reading from anywhere they have an Internet connection.

The vision for the project was to have the online system available from every public library in the state, at no cost to the libraries. One of the priorities of the Massachusetts Board of Library Commissioners (MBLC) that year was outreach to parents of young children, so the newly named ReadsinMA.org website became one of the vehicles to meeting that high-priority goal. The MBLC paid for the project as a three-year pilot using federal funds available through the Library Services and Technology Act. The site was launched in time for the start of 2007 summer reading programs, making Massachusetts the first state to do a statewide online reading program.

Each library that chooses to use the site and system receives training, support, and a unique page that is linked from the ReadsinMA.org domain for their programs. The system is available year-round, so libraries can run fall, winter, and spring programs, as well as special programs for Teen Read Week, National Children's Book Week, or other celebrations. They can have multiple programs running at once, and for different age groups, which has opened up possibilities for many libraries to add new reading programs all year. Patrons who use the program can log their reading via their online reading log, write reviews, rate books, and be entered for drawings at their libraries. They can participate from anywhere in the world where they have an Internet connection. One librarian commented on her end-of-summer evaluation, "At our party to end the Summer Reading Program, I asked the teens if they liked it and if they thought it was something that should be continued in the future. All said they loved it, and one teen said she logged in her books while on vacation, in China!" Another librarian said, "Many, many parents really appreciated having the hours online, so that they could stop by the library on the spur of the moment—from the beach or wherever—and not haul the paper logs with them everywhere."

The license terms allow every public library in the state to have access to the system. Six school districts in each regional library system also have licenses to use the system. Schools tend to run their programs during the school year, focusing on the state's children's choice book award, the Massachusetts Children's Book Award. Other schools have used the program to have students track their reading toward charitable reading programs for Heifer International or other charities. Many school and public libraries have used ReadsinMA to offer collaborative programs. By sharing log-in information and attending training together, they are able to offer exciting and interesting programs.

The Douglas Public Schools are an excellent example. Every school librarian attended training with the Douglas Public Library staff to learn how to set up and manage an online program. The staff immediately began planning how to integrate the ReadsinMA system into the schools' required summer reading assignments. Each grade now has its own separate program on the public library's ReadsinMA page, with the summer reading list posted prominently. The program allows students to read their required books and enter a short review. Students have to turn in written assignments during the first week of school to their teachers and use the ReadsinMA system to keep track of their reading as they finish each book.

Public and school librarians in the towns of Northborough and Southborough got together a few years ago to plan a special grant project. Their students enjoyed participating in the state's children's choice book award, but the librarians wanted a project that was more local. They brainstormed a list of books and, with some grant funds, started the Northborough-Southborough Children's Book Award. Each year, librarians collaborate on a list of twenty books for elementary-level readers. Students have three to four months to read the books and must read at least three to be eligible to vote. Quite a few teachers use at least one of the books in the curriculum or as a read-aloud. Tracking of the titles they read can be done on paper or through the Northborough ReadsinMA page. The librarians also work together to promote the program via fliers, bookmarks, and links on all their websites. Funding for the project has come from local grants (including the Scholastic Literacy Partnership, a nonprofit organization whose mission is to support literacy efforts of organizations nationwide), which allowed the libraries to give copies of the books on the list directly to the students. All the librarians involved plan to continue the project into the future.

Moving toward paperless online reading programs has been exciting and rewarding for librarians and library users in Massachusetts. Statistics show that, too: in 2007, 170 of 347 Massachusetts public libraries offered online programs. Of all Summer Reading Program participants, 18 percent (slightly less than twenty thousand patrons) participated online. That number shot up to 34 percent, or more than thirty-five thousand participants, in 2008, when 235 of 349 libraries had online participation, and it is expected to increase even more in 2009 when 252 libraries have online programs. Because of patron usage and positive comments from librarians, the program will continue into the future.

About the Author

Maureen Ambrosino is youth services consultant at the Central Massachusetts Regional Library System, where she helped implement the nation's first statewide online summer reading program. With her publication of "Metamorphosis," *School Library Journal* dubbed her a "raging library activist," and *Library Journal* named her a 2009 Mover and Shaker. She recently completed a Year of the Teen project that energized young-adult programming in Massachusetts. She has worked in rural, suburban, and urban libraries in three states. She is active in the Young Adult Library Services Association and other library associations in New England. Maureen can be contacted at maureen ambrosino@gmail.com.

BLAST School Outreach Program

Georgene DeFilippo

Established as a public trust in 1895, Carnegie Library of Pittsburgh (CLP) serves the citizens of Pittsburgh and Allegheny County with a distinguished history of leadership among the country's great public libraries. The CLP consists of nineteen neighborhood locations, including Main Library and the Library for the Blind and Physically Handicapped. Each year the library provides more than six thousand free programs, classes, and other learning and training opportunities that are tailored to meet the dynamic and diverse needs of western Pennsylvania residents. In addition to programs and direct services, CLP is a member of the Allegheny County Library Association and serves as a district library center for all public libraries in Allegheny County and neighboring counties.

DESCRIPTION OF COLLABORATION

In the spring of 2002, CLP, in collaboration with the Pittsburgh Public School District, developed a school outreach program called BLAST (Bringing Libraries and School Together). The original focus of the program was to provide schools with additional material resources and to offer curriculum support through interactive read-alouds and hands-on activities.

At the start of the 2003 school year, Literacy Plus, the school district's literacy initiative, asked CLP to expand the program. It was agreed that CLP staff would offer age-appropriate interactive read-aloud sessions with students in third-grade classrooms. Schools selected to receive the programs were identified as low-achieving schools as measured by the Pennsylvania System of School Assessments. In addition to the third-grade read-aloud programs, BLAST developed thematic programs for all K–5 classrooms.

Currently, BLAST creates two new thematic programs every other month, one for students in grades K–2 and another for grades 3–5. Programs for older students generally include nonfiction books and hands-on activities, and programs for the younger grades tend to be traditional library storytimes. The BLAST thematic programs are often presented in the school library. Also, BLAST is actively involved in the summer extended-year program, which runs for four to five weeks during the summer months, giving reading and math support for students reading below grade level. Moreover, BLAST provides summer reading programs in the schools and enrolls all of the children in the library's summer reading program. Students borrow books each week. During the last week of the program, they keep the final book they select.

HOW THEY GOT TOGETHER

The CLP's youth services coordinator strongly believes in collaborating with the Pittsburgh public schools. Several opportunities presented themselves in which public library staff were asked to support teacher trainings, provide booklists, and make recommendations for age-appropriate materials. After successfully meeting these challenges, the program officers for Literacy Plus approached the library, asking for reading support for the third grade classes. The program officers targeted this grade level because they believed that the high percentage of struggling readers in third grade would benefit the most from the BLAST program. Currently, third-grade teachers' share reading strategies that they are focusing on for the school year and ask BLAST staff to model these practices. Teachers have commented that BLAST's support of what they are teaching strengthens the students' understanding and comprehension of a variety of reading strategies.

LOCATIONS

The third-grade programs are held in the classroom, which enables teachers to scaffold student learning by connecting curriculum and classroom experiences. As part of this program, students are bused to their local neighborhood library in the spring. During the visit, third graders get a tour of the library, participate in an interactive read-aloud, and create a book.

The thematic programs are generally offered in the school library to ensure and strengthen school and public library partnerships. School librarians often pull books from their shelves that support the BLAST theme and encourage children to read more about the topic. Topics for thematic programs have included inventors, music, Australia, weather, and a variety of animals. These topics often do not get enough exposure in the curriculum; teachers and librarians support the thematic programs because they provide students with background knowledge on science, geography, and social studies in addition to reading and math skills, which are the major focus in the classroom.

AGE LEVEL AND SIZE OF AUDIENCE

The third-grade programs are offered to the schools where the greatest percentage of students scored below the basic range on the Pennsylvania System of School Assessment. Last year BLAST provided the third-grade programs in sixteen elementary schools (thirty-eight classrooms) and served seven hundred children.

The thematic programs are offered to students in grades K–5. Letters are sent to school principals, who make the connection or forward the information to their school librarian, reading coach, or teacher responsible for program visits. In the last school year (2008–2009) BLAST presented 355 programs to 12,225 students in the Pittsburgh public schools.

PUBLICITY

Letters were sent every other month to the school principals inviting them to sign up for the thematic programs. The BLAST staff developed a bookmark for teachers that promotes the programs with both website and phone information. An e-newsletter has also been developed for elementary educators, providing ideas for programs, resources, and websites that elementary teachers can find useful for program planning. Teachers can view program outlines and book-lists at the BLAST website (www.carnegielibrary.org/blast/). Also, BLAST has presented numerous workshops both locally and statewide to share information about the importance of informational text in the primary classroom and to demonstrate interactive read-alouds and reader's theater.

STAFFING AND EQUIPMENT

The BLAST staff consists of two certified elementary teachers. Staff are recent college graduates who bring their knowledge of literacy instruction and classroom dynamics into each outreach program.

Each year, ten books are chosen for the third-grade read-aloud program. Three years ago, after reading about the importance of informational text in the primary classroom, three nonfiction or informational texts were added to the program. Currently, the third-grade program has three informational books and seven narrative books used for read-alouds. During the past two years, a book of poetry was added to expand the genre selection in the read-aloud program.

After the read-aloud, one hardback copy of the book is given to the school library and another is left in the classroom. This collection of quality multicultural texts enhances the classroom library and allows students the opportunity to go back and reread the book.

Writing is also a strong component of the program. Students are given a blank book at the beginning of the school year in which they can record reflective responses to the books read aloud or draw pictures as their response to the text. This process allows students to respond in whichever way is most comfortable for them and is respectful of differences in learning styles.

For the thematic programs, a variety of age-appropriate books are brought into the classroom to engage and motivate the children to read. The programs are highly interactive and complement the elementary curriculum.

PROGRAM OBJECTIVES

- Enhance the reading attitudes and abilities of third-grade students
- Provide equitable access to public library resources and materials
- Increase visibility of Carnegie Library of Pittsburgh in the elementary classroom

HANDOUTS AND CHECKLISTS

The BLAST staff developed a teacher contract that sets forth BLAST's expectations of teachers and what teachers can expect from BLAST. A teachers' handout includes ways to expand the story in the classroom, an activity sheet for children with writing prompts, a reading skill activity, and additional information on the book or author, and trivia.

THINGS TO CONSIDER

School districts often undergo reorganizations and administrative staff changes. Consider beginning each year with a dialogue and commitment from the administrators of the elementary school programs. (In Pittsburgh, there was initially a lot of explanation about the program; now the BLAST name is very recognizable and represents quality programs.)

The program strongly supports the Pennsylvania academic standards, and the standards are listed on the teacher handouts.

The BLAST program provides the opportunity for library staff to develop personal connections with the students and thus build on a library relationship.

The BLAST program has made a consistent effort to remain a reliable constant in the school lives of the children served by the program.

The BLAST program is purposeful in both program planning and
book selection.

Consider a reading specialist to evaluate the program. In the first five
years of the program, BLAST engaged Dr. Rita Bean, a reading
specialist at the University of Pittsburgh, to evaluate the BLAST
program.

FUNDING

Funding is an ongoing challenge. Initially, BLAST was funded by the Grable
Foundation for three years and then renewed for another three years. The
program also received support from the Pittsburgh Foundation and the Claude
Benedum Foundation. The Benedum Foundation asked the BLAST program
to run a pilot study in a more rural area of Pennsylvania to see whether the successful urban school program would be successful elsewhere. The BLAST staff
trained the local children's librarian to do the interactive read-aloud program
with third-grade students. The library was able to secure funding the following
year from a local bank to continue the program.

Currently, the library receives support for the BLAST program from Educational Improvement Tax Credit funding. Businesses in Pennsylvania can
pay their taxes to the state through this educational support program. For the
last four years, Pittsburgh Public Schools have also provided financial support
for the BLAST program. Their contribution covers the books purchased for
the classrooms, the bus trips, and miscellaneous and consumable materials,
including incentives and other materials to support the thematic programs.

About the Author

Georgene DeFilippo is youth services coordinator for Carnegie Library of Pittsburgh. She plans, coordinates, and implements systemwide programs, col-
laborates with Pittsburgh Public Schools, and develops partnerships and
collaborations with local agencies that serve children throughout Pittsburgh.
She is a member of the American Library Association, the Association for
Library Services for Children, the Public Library Association, the International Reading Association, and the National Association for the Education
of Young Children. She participated on the 2009 Caldecott Committee and
the 2004 Newbery Committee. She has also served a variety of local and
statewide library organizations. Georgene can be reached at defilippog@
carnegielibrary.org.

BLAST Outreach Service Agreement

2008–2009

We are really looking forward to visiting your classroom to promote literacy and the love of reading this school year! The purpose of this agreement is to clarify what you can expect from our service this school year, and what we can expect from you. Please read and sign both copies of this agreement; you may keep the other copy for your personal records.

BLAST Responsibilities

- Schedule a minimum of ten visits per classroom throughout the school year.
- Facilitate one field trip to the Carnegie Library for each classroom.
- Provide a literacy-rich experience for both teachers and students through multicultural interactive read-alouds and informational text exploration read-alouds.
- Enhance the classroom library by providing new and diverse literature, as well as two vocabulary words to accompany every book.
- Provide activity sheets to teachers, which will consist of extension activities for students (to do inside or outside of school).
- Provide students with a journal to complete a writing activity following each read-aloud.
- Assessments (student attitude and student interview) will be conducted throughout the school year to collect data for the ongoing BLAST program evaluation.

Third-Grade Classroom Teacher's Responsibilities

- Contact BLAST team member in case of a cancellation.
- Actively participate in the program to indicate support and validate credibility of this program.
- Fill out BLAST questionnaires and evaluations throughout the school year.
- If necessary, assist students or BLAST member with any assessments and the journal project.
- Display books and vocabulary in the classroom, providing easy access to students.

Inclement Weather and Cancellations

If we cannot make a scheduled visit for any reason, we will be sure to notify you ASAP. If a session is cancelled, we will make every effort to reschedule immediately. In the event of a school delay, the visit will be rescheduled.

We look forward to having a terrific year with both you and your students!

Please note: Your signature confirms that you have read this agreement and concur to the terms of service. After receiving your signed agreement we will begin scheduling for the school year.

Name of Third-Grade Teacher: _____

Date: _____

Name of BLAST Team Member: _____ Date: _____

10

Braille That Stands Out in More Ways Than One

Deborah J. Margolis

The Maryland State Library for the Blind and Physically Handicapped (MDLBPH) is a regional library of the Library of Congress's National Library Service for the Blind and Physically Handicapped. The MDLBPH is administered and funded through the Maryland State Department of Education's Division of Library Development and Services (DLDS). The library has an active and supportive Friends of the Library group. The MDLBPH serves any Maryland resident who is unable to read standard print. This includes blind people and people with low vision, people with reading disabilities like dyslexia, and people who have had strokes and other physical disabilities that prevent reading printed material. The library's collection contains materials in audio format, Braille, large print, and described video and DVD. In addition to these formats, the children's collection includes picture books with translucent Braille pages, called print-Braille or twin-vision books.

The library had a small children's area in a back corner, named for June H. Kleeman, a friend of the library who was passionate about library children's services. Most of the library's children's books, including the most colorful and attractive print-Braille books, were housed in closed stacks three floors below. A new youth services coordinator, Deborah Margolis, thought that the children's materials should be brought front and center into the atriumlike reading area, and the library director, Jill Lewis, agreed from the start.

Margolis had heard about community-based design projects through her sister-in-law, a faculty member in graphic design at Carnegie Mellon University. Margolis contacted the Maryland Institute College of Art (MICA) graphic design chair to see whether there might be a student who would want to work on a new children's area at MDLBPH. As fate would have it, Lindsey

Muir, a graduate student in graphic design at MICA, had been contacting area organizations to develop a master's thesis project working with blind children.

Their goal was to create a beautiful, interactive, multisensory library children's area that would be a destination for families, parents, and teachers, both sighted and vision impaired. In addition, because only 10 percent of blind adults read Braille and only 10 percent of blind children are being taught Braille, the library and the designer wanted to promote Braille—and the library's Braille collections—in the new space.

Muir wanted to know what graphic design felt like to the touch. Her research consisted of personal interviews with the families of twelve young library patrons whom the children's librarian referred. They included families with blind and low-vision children, children with multiple disabilities, and families with a visually impaired parent. By going to the families' homes, Muir learned various ways that families cope with blindness. As one can imagine, simple things—such as tying a shoelace or lighting a match—are challenging to someone who cannot see. Muir also visited local organizations for the blind to see how they designed their spaces. She learned that adding different floor textures—carpet versus tile—helps people navigate through a room. She also found out that furniture with rounded edges helped prevent people from being injured.

Muir discovered that almost every family was interested in two components: learning Braille in an easy and fun way and using sound components to draw people into the environment. In response, she created a Braille learning station with a negative Braille cell made from Plexiglas. A child would then be able to place a ball in one of the six cells to build a letter in Braille. In addition to this Braille learning station, the designer created tactile animals made out of textiles resembling animal furs and hides. She included large red push buttons, or switches, that trigger the sound of the corresponding animal. In between Braille cells and the animals, Muir created a horizontal stripe of wildly different textured and colored fabrics, including blue "Cookie Monster fur," green Astroturf, and yellow raincoat.

The multisensory wall was painted in stripes of bright, high-contrast colors, which some people with low vision could see. Muir's interest in typography and desire to make a statement about the importance of Braille led her to design a massive graphic of bright-blue vinyl circles spelling out "read Braille." Muir tested the height of the pieces to be installed on the wall with children to be sure that each level was hung appropriately for children to reach.

PUBLICITY

At MICA, Lindsey Muir had a thesis show, which was featured on the MICA website. Muir also spoke about the project at numerous campus events. The library planned a dedication ceremony to unveil the new children's area, which served as the major vehicle for publicity. All library patrons were mailed an invitation in Braille or large print featuring the design. The invitation was sent electronically to the library's electronic discussion board, to the friends and advisory boards, and to professional contacts in the Maryland library world and beyond. The marketing specialist for the library's parent organization, DLDS, crafted a press release in anticipation of the dedication ceremony. After the children's area was complete, the design of the children's area was featured on the library's website, its kids' website, and on youth services handouts. Tours of the June H. Kleeman Children's Reading Area are available on an ongoing basis and can be tailored to an individual or group's interest.

STAFF AND EQUIPMENT

Muir donated her time, as all her work designing the library space was part of her yearlong master's thesis project. She spent innumerable hours planning and executing every detail of the children's area and children's website. She installed the Braille learning center and supervised the painting and installation of the vinyl Braille dots on the walls.

Although the designer's time was free, the library staff spent considerable time working on the redesign project. The youth services coordinator was in very frequent contact with the designer. The library director was consulted periodically as challenges arose or when major decisions needed approval. The library staff and advisory board were consulted on the overall design.

The Braille Learning Station.

Marisa Conner, youth services administrator at Baltimore County Public Library, volunteered her time to visit MDLBPH and consult with Muir and Margolis. She had recently been involved in the creation of Storyville, a very successful interactive children's environment at the county library that was an inspiration for this project.

Painting of the walls with different stripes of bright color and the application of large vinyl circles on the walls was more staff intensive than had been anticipated. The library's building maintenance company, Abacus, donated time of facilities staff. When the yellow color painted on the multisensory wall was just too bright, even repellent to some, it was difficult to ask Abacus to come back and repaint. When the laser level used to line up the vinyl dots peeled paint off the adjacent wall, and it needed to be repainted, it was again a tense situation, especially when the dedication ceremony was approaching and the rental of a boom lift was necessary to reapply the dots! Through delicate communications and the close involvement of the designer in the installation, all turned out well. The Abacus account manager came to the dedication ceremony and Abacus was acknowledged in writing on the program.

In-house maintenance staff assembled furniture and cleaned the area. They disassembled and repackaged a table and chairs that turned out to be too small. Muir and Margolis found that there is more design furniture on the market for toddlers than for school-aged kids.

The library's Braille specialist advised on the use of Braille in the installation and collaborated on the relocation of Braille books from the closed stacks to the new children's area. Information technology staff prepared and installed the accessible computer workstation (accessible software included JAWS, Zoom-Text, Inspiration, and Kidspiration). Other library staff members prepared the digital audiobook players available for use in the children's area. The library's secretary made preparations for the dedication ceremony.

COSTS

The project cost about $7,000 for supplies and furniture. This project was funded solely by the Friends of the Maryland State Library for the Blind and Physically Handicapped. Margolis and Muir proposed the design to the friends board, bringing designs and prototypes. They were granted $5,000 for the project. The youth services portion of the Friends of the Library's budget covered surplus costs.

PURCHASES

A comfortable, welcoming couch where parents and children could curl up together and read was a priority. This was the most expensive purchase, costing about $2,000. The couch is modern, rounded, soft (microsuede polyester), and extremely durable (purchased from Room and Board). Muir made throw pillows for the couch out of some of the same fabrics used on the multisensory wall.

Other furniture included a children's computer desk that seats two children on a bench (Wild Zoo), a chair for a parent to also work with the children at the computer (Crate and Barrel), a round table (Pottery Barn) and chairs suitable for school-aged children (Land of Nod), and a comfortable adult-sized chair (IKEA). Two contemporary children's step stools were purchased so that even the youngest children could reach the animals (Snap Step). Finally, the designer identified and purchased two round ottomans made of brightly colored strips of soft rubber flip-flop material (Design within Reach). These ottomans can be sat on or rolled on by children and are of great interest to all ages and abilities.

Toys for young children were purchased, including wooden blocks with print and Braille letters (National Federation of the Blind Independence Market), magnetic letters in print and Braille (National Federation of the Blind Independence Market), wooden lacing beads and wooden cars (Holgate Toys), sensory balls (Lakeshore Learning), and Audubon birds (stuffed-animal birds that make real bird sounds), as were bins for holding the toys (Community Playthings). Several companies graciously agreed to sell their products at a wholesale or discounted price, or at least offer free shipping.

Two Victor Reader Stream digital audiobook players were purchased at a discount from the manufacturer (HumanWare) for use in the new children's area.

SPECIAL HANDOUTS AND USEFUL CHECKLISTS

Muir designed a children's website for MDLBPH. For one section of the website, she interviewed three adult patrons with guide dogs and wrote biographies of the dogs. The website also includes a history of Louis Braille, recommended books, and a Braille word for the day (www.lbph.lib.md.us/kids/). Muir designed a font incorporating print and Braille. She created letterpress bookmarks (hand pressed) to distribute at her thesis show and at the library dedication ceremony. In addition, Muir designed signage with the words "June H. Kleeman Children's Reading Area" in the font. Braille tactile polyurethane dots were added to make the sign accessible to Braille readers (3M).

THINGS TO KEEP IN MIND

- Gain support from the library director and library board or other key political players very early on in the process.
- Have one library contact person for the community partner.

- Be in frequent communication with the partner. The designer and the youth services coordinator were in contact every few days for the MDLBPH project.
- Be respectful of the expertise of your library's partner and other professionals involved in the project. They will have a different point of view and different goals, deadlines, and sensitivities. If working with a student intern, remember that this may be his or her first real-world work experience.
- Involve staff, boards, vendors, and service providers in the excitement of the project.
- Have a color model of the design for those involved to see and feel.
- Ask vendors or service providers for donations or discounts.
- Test paint colors on as large a sample area as possible.
- Look beyond the furniture vendors that cater to libraries.
- Make sure furniture is the size that you need; measure heights and compare specs.
- Honor your library's partners.
- Publicly thank all key contributors, if they wish to be acknowledged publicly.
- Have a dedication ceremony to publicize the new space.
- Continue to publicize after the project is done.

Lindsey Muir's newly created Braille font.

About the Author

Deborah J. Margolis has worked as a librarian in public, academic, and specialized libraries. She earned her MLS at Syracuse University and has an MA in Jewish studies. Deborah was assistant manager of information services at the Enoch Pratt Free Library, where she served as liaison to Maryland's statewide virtual reference service, Maryland AskUsNow! At MDLBPH, Deborah adapted the Mother Goose on the Loose program to be more inclusive of children with special needs. She currently is an independent library consultant, working on projects including grant writing and inclusive children's programming. Deborah lives in Michigan and can be contacted at djmargolis@hotmail.com.

four

Children's and Play Museums and Public Libraries

Party with Your Partners

Plan a Kids' Book Fest!

Starr LaTronica

The Four County Library System (FCLS; www.4CLS.org) is an administrative organization that provides consolidated services to forty-two member libraries in upstate New York. As the youth services and outreach manager, I am a big believer in collaboration with people and entities outside of the library. In 1995, as the mother of then two-year-old twins and a first grader, I was excited by the creative environments and thoughtful activities available at the Discovery Center of the Southern Tier in Binghamton, New York (www.thediscoverycenter.org). I subsequently approached the Discovery Center director with a proposition to promote its programs within the network of libraries, hoping in return to receive guest passes for participants in the Summer Reading Program. One thing quickly led to another, and the Discovery Center and the libraries enjoyed several joint projects.

It was at the Cabin Fever Festival in Ithaca, New York, that the FCLS discovered the Family Reading Partnership (FRP), an organization that is dedicated to creating a culture of literacy by providing quality books to all families in Tompkins County (www.familyreading.org). Among its many efforts to imbue the community with a love of books and reading, FRP hosts a free, daylong festival of authors; illustrators; and hands-on, book related activities and performances. Community organizations and businesses join together to transform the local middle school into a literary landscape. After having attended and assisted with a few such festivals, I wanted to bring the experience back to my own community through FCLS.

My cohorts at the Discovery Center were just as enthusiastic. They secured an empty storefront at the local mall, a central location and one that would ensure a built-in audience. We planned the event for a Saturday in late November to coincide with chilly weather, the beginning of holiday shopping, and the timing of Children's Book Week. As with any good collaborative effort, we began by phoning friends. We enlisted child-care councils, early education partners, and other agencies that serve families. The local authors Suzanne Bloom, Lois Grambling, David Kirk, and Liz Rosenberg donated their time, as did a host of high-profile members of the community who volunteered to be guest readers. Comfortable furniture (which I donated!) established a cozy reading area. The vacant retail space was filled with vibrant color, thanks to friends at FRP who loaned costumes and decor, including an eighteen-foot sculpture of Eric Carle's Very Hungry Caterpillar and a huge interactive fabric version of the same. Ta-da! The first festival, Going Buggy with Books, was an exhilarating extravaganza.

In retrospect, FCLS realized that the most labor-intensive part of the project had been transporting materials and transforming an empty space into a family-friendly, attractive environment for a single day. They realized that that environment already existed at the Discovery Center, where there was already an established cozy reading corner. We had been so impressed with FRP's efforts and so intent on replicating their success that we had overlooked their own valuable resources. Later, with flexibility firmly in mind, it was time to establish the event that would best suit our circumstances and community.

It took two years before we were ready for the next book fest. The Discovery Center generously agreed to grant free admission to all families presenting a library card, with costs to be recouped through sales in its café and gift shop. The FCLS recruited participating agencies and authors, funding any honorarium fees through book sales and grants. Both agencies solicited volunteers from staff, families, volunteer organizations, and the local university. The FRP continued its support through the loan of book-character costumes and huge banners with full-color picture-book art that proclaimed "Read to me. Any time, any place."

In addition to the initial roster of community partners, the library branched out to school groups, school librarians, drama departments, museums, and the local storytelling guild. As the list of participating partners grew, so did the possibilities. Each new contact brought fresh ideas and resources. The Susquehanna Storytellers decided to hold their Tellabration event. A local high school drama club developed a performance piece based on nursery rhymes. Barnes and Noble supplied a wealth of promotional items (e.g., small toys, lunch boxes), as did area libraries.

Local authors generously agreed to a return engagement to read and sign their books at various intervals throughout the day. Daniel Mahoney, the author and illustrator of *The Saturday Escape* (Clarion, 2002), a delightful story of three friends who sneak out of the house and away from their responsibilities to attend storytime at the library, accepted our invitation to escape to the Discovery Center on a Saturday for a day of reading fun. Daniel presented a slide show, drawing demonstration, and reading in the morning and then conducted a free workshop on creating a picture book to the first twenty-five children aged ten and up who registered in advance. In between events, he signed books and chatted graciously with fans. His honorarium was affordable, as FCLS had helped to negotiate his appearance at several area schools earlier in the week.

Promotion was conducted through the local school district outlets (e.g., school newsletters), appearance on local television-news shows, and the Discovery Center newsletter. A feature article profiling Daniel Mahoney and the event appeared in full color on the front page of the "Lifestyles" section of the newspaper two days prior to the event. There was a crowd waiting for the doors to open Saturday morning and a steady stream of attendance that totaled nearly 350 families over the course of the day.

The participating agencies recognized the festival as a valuable outreach opportunity. Each hosted a book-related activity for children and distributed information on their programs and services to attending adults. The local museum helped children create bird-shaped books and distributed their schedule for upcoming children's art classes, and school librarians provided materials to fashion bookmarks and information on the importance of reading and school libraries. The local PBS station showed videos of its literary programming while conducting an alphabet I Spy game and handing out information on media literacy. The early childhood council offered opportunities to enhance a number of early literacy skills with children while educating their parents and caregivers on the importance and effectiveness of the activities. Of course, libraries promoted their programs and resources and distributed basic information on locations and schedules.

Throughout the day, volunteer readers presented picture books to attendees, and costumed book characters roamed the site. Families traveled through a variety of exhibit environments on a treasure hunt based on *The Saturday Escape*, designed by the talented staff at the Discovery Center. All attendees were encouraged to take home a book from the gently used children's book exchange. Books had been collected for this purpose, and the exchange had been promoted in the publicity so that families could bring books to contribute as well.

It was a fruitful day for both the families and the exhibitors, and the Kids' Bookfest had securely taken root in the community. Since then, the event has flourished and has become an annual occurrence. We continue to cultivate partnerships with community agencies and funders. Grants from Barnes and Noble and our state senator have provided support for featured author appearances and workshops.

Some of the less successful offshoots of the fest have been pruned away. Through experience, we have streamlined the planning process and we need fewer volunteers. We noted that kids didn't really like to sit still and listen to stories for an extended period of time when they have a fabulous children's museum and a host of creative activities at their disposal—and they are generally unimpressed by local dignitaries. Thus, we reduced the number of storytelling sessions and celebrity readers and saved them for another time and place.

About the Author

Starr LaTronica began her career at the Berkeley Public Library in California and is currently youth services and outreach manager for FCLS in upstate New York. She has served on the board of directors of the Association for Library Service to Children and as president of the Youth Services Section of the New York Library Association. As the namesake of Daniel Pinkwater's librarian in *Looking for Bobowiscz* and *The Artsy Smartsy Club,* she strives to live up to Starr Lakawanna's proclamation, "I live to astonish, amaze, and astound. Those are things librarians do well." Starr can be reached at starrbooks@hotmail.com.

Borrow a Book . . . at the Museum!

Carol Sandler

The Strong National Museum of Play in Rochester, New York, is the only museum in the world devoted solely to the study of play and is the second-largest children's museum in the country. Strong is also home to the National Toy Hall of Fame, the International Center for the History of Electronic Games, and the *American Journal of Play*. Grounded by the world's largest and most comprehensive collection of toys, dolls, games, and play-related artifacts, the museum explores the cultural history of play to encourage learning, creativity, and discovery through its exhibits, programs, events, and publications.

Located approximately a quarter mile from Strong National Museum of Play is the Central Library of Rochester and Monroe County. Central is one of eleven city branch libraries that constitute Rochester Public Library, and it is the headquarters of both Rochester Public Library and the Monroe County Library System. Founded in 1954, the Monroe County Library System is a federation of twenty independent public libraries that includes the city branches and the town libraries located in Monroe County. Like the Strong National Museum of Play, the Monroe County Library System is chartered by the New York State Board of Regents. Although the museum regularly attracts guests from outside the Rochester Metropolitan Statistical Area, the majority of visitation and memberships comes from within the greater Rochester area, largely serving the same population as Rochester Public Library and the Monroe County Library System. The five-county region serves a diverse population of more than 1 million people and more than 260,000 families.

Both Strong National Museum of Play and Rochester Public Library embrace a culture of collaboration in their separate spheres. Both organizations were open to the idea of a partnership that would benefit both institutions and the community they serve. Their close proximity in the metropolitan center of Rochester, their cultural ties, and their commitment to provide educational and recreational programming and services of exceptional quality to diverse audiences united them in their missions and visions. Prior to 1998, the two institutions collaborated on a limited scale to place small collections of Central's books into exhibits for reference, to distribute information on museum programs and exhibits, and to participate jointly in the Culture Is Fun project. Both the success and the limitations of those endeavors informed discussions of the potential for a stronger, more effective relationship.

Founded in 1968 by Margaret Woodbury Strong, the museum began as a history museum. Its mission has advanced through a process of intense scrutiny and evaluation to better understand its audience and to provide the highest quality and variety of experiences and services attainable. Throughout the 1980s and early 1990s, a progressive series of focus groups, visitor surveys, and market studies were undertaken, each encompassing an ever-larger radius extending beyond the Rochester Metropolitan Statistical Area. The studies concluded that the museum's primary audience consisted of families with children who were seeking a cultural experience that was both educational and fun. As a result, new interactive exhibits were introduced that were highly hands-on, and complementary programs were developed that targeted primarily families with children.

In 1997, an initial expansion added an atrium entrance with a vintage diner and carousel; a Sesame Street exhibit, built in collaboration with Children's Television Workshop (now Sesame Workshop); and Super Kids Market, built in collaboration with Wegmans Food Markets, an enormously popular supermarket chain. These efforts were rewarded as attendance rose to three hundred thousand and membership rose to seven thousand families. The success of all the initiatives to advance the museum's appeal to families with children encouraged the museum to pursue creative, new approaches to enhance its services.

G. Rollie Adams, the president and chief executive officer of Strong National Museum of Play, and Richard Panz, the director of Rochester Public Library, initiated discussions between the two organizations. Teams from both institutions met to explore common interests, goals, and realities. Both institutions have a commitment to reach out to the community to provide the resources and innovative programming that will educate, inform, and entertain. Each institution possesses strengths that are both unique and complementary. The museum has its singular collections, interactive and engaging exhibits, educational programs, and special events. Services provided by the Monroe County Library System include circulation, shipping and delivery, consultant and advisory services, interlibrary loan, an online public-access catalog, and promotion. Proving the adage that the "whole is greater than the sum of its parts," this system of collaboration between independent libraries allows each to maintain its unique identity within its community while providing every member of the community, of every age, with equal access to a full range of resources, activities, and programs that are both recreational and instructive. The library also has extensive resources, a vital children's center, a state-of-the-art computer network, and electronic services accessible twenty-four hours a day, seven days a week, via the Internet, as well as educational programs, activities and special events, and a well-developed customer base. Both institutions were looking for new ways to enhance the downtown neighborhood; build on the strengths of each organization; employ technology to engage and entertain; and target services to special population groups, families, and children.

The goals for this project were identified as follows: to promote literacy and reading among children and families, to increase opportunities to access and use services, to enhance guest activity options at Strong, to increase public visibility of both Central and Strong, and to improve the image of downtown as a family destination. Linking reading to activities that are novel and imaginative, fun and meaningful, educational and playful, and in an environment that is nonthreatening and supportive, establishes a foundation for lifelong learning. To achieve this ideal, it was decided that books would be integrated directly into museum exhibits. This had been tried previously, but this time there were two significant prerequisites: the books would circulate and the majority of books would be targeted to children between the ages of three and twelve. It was determined that the best and most efficient means to circulate books would be to take advantage of the state-of-the-art technology, experience, quality, and familiarity offered through Rochester Public Library and the Monroe County Library System. To achieve this, in 1999, the museum contracted with Rochester Public Library to become a mini-branch of Central. Through this contract, which is renewed every three years, the museum fully funds the library, paying for all services provided by Central. Funding to establish the library was provided through a generous gift to the museum from Grada Hopeman Gelser and her family of more than $1 million, and the library is named in her honor.

The services made available by Central and mentioned previously enable the museum to offer guests all of the benefits provided by Rochester Public Library and the Monroe County Library System. Guests can use their Monroe County Public Library card to borrow books located in museum exhibits, to return books to this library or to any library in the Monroe County Library System, to access the online public-access catalog and their accounts at terminals located throughout the museum, and to get a library card at the museum's centrally located circulation desk. Children in kindergarten can get their own cards as long as a parent or guardian signs their application. As a mini-branch, the museum is obligated to follow the same rules and procedures set forth by Rochester Public Library and the Monroe County Library System. However, one exception to the card system was made to accommodate museum members who live outside of Monroe County. For nonresidents, there is a free restricted card that allows them to borrow books only from Strong or a $30 annual fee for the public library card.

Within the museum, the Grada Hopeman Gelser Library is administered collaboratively by two operating teams, the library team and the guest services team. Carol Sandler, director of the research library and archives, is the primary liaison with Central and is responsible for selecting the books to be integrated with the exhibits. In this task, she is assisted by a contractual agreement with Rochester Public Library, which provides the professional assistance of one of Central's children's librarians. Because a majority of the books are targeted to children between the ages of three and twelve, this benefit is of critical importance. A special team of library hosts is selected from within the museum guest services team. In addition to the extensive guest services training they receive, the hosts receive additional, specialized library training. They are responsible for staffing the circulation desk, assisting guests, returning books to their proper locations in the exhibits, and making sure that the books are appealingly presented. Much of the circulating library's success depends on the ready availability and direct appeal of having the books integrated with the exhibits. Rarely do guests come to the museum looking for specific titles. However, once they are there and discover the books, there is a strong impulse to borrow them. The experience is much like that of going into a bookstore and coming out with an armload of books, with the added benefit that there is no charge to borrow them. It is hoped that the positive and rewarding experience of borrowing books will instill a lifelong love for reading, libraries, and museums.

In 2006, the museum doubled in size to 282,000 square feet of new and renovated exhibit space. A new wing was added to house two new permanent exhibits that celebrate books and reading. The largest, Reading Adventureland, occupies twelve thousand square feet and invites guests into five imaginary literary landscapes of mystery, fantasy, nonsense, fairy tales, and adventure. The second exhibit, The Berenstain Bears Down a Sunny Dirt Road, created in partnership with the Berenstain family, brings guests into a world that comes straight from the pages of the beloved Berenstain Bears books. In conjunction with both of these highly interactive and imaginative exhibits, the museum's education team developed a menu of lessons, activities, and events for age groups ranging from preschool to adult that integrate play and learning with reading. Clifford, Arthur, and Curious George have also made guest appearances in exhibits borrowed from other museums.

Success is measured by more than numbers—although numbers are reassuring. In 2008, attendance surged to more than 560,000 guests, and membership grew to more than 17,170 households. During the ten years of the library and museum collaboration, library book circulation in the museum has grown from 6,821 in 2000 (the first full year of operation) to 18,666 in 2008. With the introduction of new exhibitions, lessons, programs, and events that encourage learning, creativity, discovery, and reading, Strong National Museum of Play and Rochester Public Library continue to work together to advance their mutual goal of nurturing readers.

About the Author

Carol Sandler received her MLIS from University at Buffalo–SUNY in 1986. That same year, she began her professional library career as reference librarian and archivist for the research library of Strong National Museum of Play. She became director of library and archives in 1993. The opening of the Grada Hopeman Gelser Library in 1999 in collaboration with Rochester Public Library has added a welcome new dimension of librarianship and an even greater appreciation for the gift of libraries. Carol can be contacted at Sandler@museumofplay.org.

Countdown to Kindergarten

Jeri Robinson and Krystal Beaulieu

Conceived through a collaboration between the Boston Children's Museum, Head Start, Boston Public Schools, and the mayor's office in 1999, Boston's Countdown to Kindergarten engages families, educators, and community partners in a citywide effort to strengthen and expand early learning opportunities and to celebrate and support the transition into kindergarten, a significant educational and developmental milestone for children and their families. Through this collaborative effort, the mayor, the Boston School Committee, and the superintendent of schools are partnering with more than thirty public and private organizations, including the Boston Public Library.

Countdown to Kindergarten has a multipronged mission. Countdown hopes to ensure that Boston's families with young children take advantage of the academic and social benefits kindergarten provides by raising public awareness about the value of kindergarten, the availability of full-school-day programs, and the steps family members can take to support their child's kindergarten experience. In collaboration with its community partners, Countdown to Kindergarten aims to coordinate and expand social and learning activities that help children prepare for school and help them transition from home or preschool into kindergarten. It lays the groundwork for primary caregivers (e.g., parents, grandparents, guardians) to be active partners in their children's education at home and at school, from birth through their education in elementary school and beyond. It supports the Boston Public Schools in their work to ensure that the process of choosing schools, registering, and entering kindergarten is clear and welcoming for all families.

The Kindergarten Celebration at the Children's Museum has become a signature event for Countdown. Occurring in August each year, the celebration is the official send-off for Boston's newest kindergartners. The event is a special occasion for children and their families, providing them with an exclusive evening at the museum with free access to the Boston Children's Museum exhibits. Fun activities include climbing on school buses, playing literacy games to help learn about school readiness, and sending children home with some school supplies that will prepare them for kindergarten. Graphing games help children develop simple counting and graphing skills. For example, children added their personal information to a bar graph using squares of paper. They answered questions such as "What is your favorite color?" "In what month is your birthday?" and "What school will you be attending?" Parents are encouraged to talk with present Boston Public School staff regarding any last-minute questions about their child's new school system.

The Boston Public Library (BPL) started collaborating with Countdown to Kindergarten in its earliest days by participating in the Kindergarten Celebration. The Boston Public Library hosts a table for library card sign-ups. It often also supports the event by reading aloud to children. This has been an ongoing commitment and is a win-win situation for both partners. The collaboration costs the BPL only personnel time, after hours. Also, depending on budget, some years the library has been able to provide a free book to each child at the event.

In 2004, the library's partnership substantially grew to include their involvement in the Boston Children's Museum "I'm Going to Kindergarten" T-shirt distribution. Countdown provides each new kindergarten student with a free T-shirt, which is the child's free admission ticket to lots of fun and educational activities throughout the summer, such as trips to museums, storytimes at bookstores, swim times, and so on. The BPL's twenty-seven branches agreed to be the distribution points for the T-shirts starting in 2004. Kindergarten families were mailed a postcard inviting them into their local library to pick up their free T-shirt. The children's librarians served as contacts and were responsible for giving out the shirts, collecting postcards, and returning them to the museum for tabulation. In turn, the invitation, available in eight languages, brings new families into the libraries, where they can sign up for library cards and/or take advantage of programming.

Countdown worked with the BPL to make the T-shirt distribution more focused on school readiness. To do this, the librarians were asked to give out a readiness packet that consisted of not just the T-shirt but also the DVD *I'm Ready!* (which illustrates what kindergarten is like in Boston and how to get ready for it), as well as a summer guide, which lists all the fun, free stuff families can do together to keep young minds and bodies growing. Families must bring in a postcard that Countdown sends out to receive the packets or some other proof of assignment in a Boston Public School kindergarten, which librarians can then use as proof of address to help the family sign up for a library card. Proof of address can be the most difficult step for families signing up for cards, especially those who recently moved into Boston from other countries. For the past five years, Countdown has been able to offer incentives to libraries that work hard to promote the readiness packets, providing the three libraries with the best displays prizes for their creative efforts. These prizes are not big—usually $50 gift certificates to a local office-supply store—but they help motivate and rally a competition among the librarians.

In 2006, Countdown to Kindergarten partnered with the BPL in yet another way, working together to bring smaller, community-focused kindergarten celebrations to the many neighborhoods of Boston. Recognizing that not all five thousand kindergarten families could attend the one celebration at the Children's Museum, the idea behind the smaller events, called Kindergarten Days, was to bring celebration opportunities into the neighborhoods where families could more easily access the special opportunities to mark their children's milestone to kindergarten. The most successful Kindergarten Days bring neighborhood school principals and teachers in to meet their new students while providing parents and kindergarteners alike an opportunity to connect over their shared experience and feelings. The BPL cosponsors the special events, acting as the host site, providing storytime and/or other special activities, and identifying local resources and businesses to donate snacks and supplies. Countdown creates and mails the invitations; advertises the events in local newspapers; handles press releases; and provides a core set of activities, including face painting and arts and crafts. Countdown to Kindergarten also ensures there are volunteers to staff the event, although some library branches have done so with their friends-of-the-library organizations. Kindergarten Days have been beneficial to the librarians, too, by allowing the libraries to build a reputation as a resource for families in the neighborhood. Community members are introduced to the children's librarian and learn about his or her storytimes and other free programming.

Over the years, the library has been a constant partner behind the scenes as well, attending Countdown's bimonthly partner planning and collaboration meetings. The meetings update the partners about Countdown's activities and include brainstorming about better implementation and outreach. They also include requests for in-kind support, including human resources. The library has been a tremendous partner on this front. In 2007, Countdown began planning its Parent as a Child's First Teacher outreach campaign. The library signed on as a work-group member, providing invaluable input about content and distribution methods—again offering to display and/or distribute materials. In November 2008, when Talk, Read, Play was launched, all twenty-seven branches handed out palm cards to patrons as they walked in. The palm cards talked about the importance of talking with young children and included some simple developmental tips. This effort helped to disseminate more than seven thousand pieces of literature on the first day of the campaign!

One of the most promising aspects of Countdown to Kindergarten's collaborative relationship with the Boston Public Library is its promise for duplication, even without a local Countdown to Kindergarten or similar organization.

A Kindergarten Celebration or smaller-scale Kindergarten Days can be planned with a few simple phone calls to the school district, or even to a local school, and a local vendor. To plan these events, Countdown to Kindergarten first obtains a list of all of the incoming kindergarten students from the Boston Public Schools to mail invitations. We place reminder ads in some of Boston's neighborhoods papers, and then it is time to prepare for the children to come! There have been simpler Kindergarten Day celebrations when the children come in and enjoy face painting, temporary tattoos, coloring, and some craft activity, then enjoy a story read by the children's librarian or a performance by some musician or magician with which the librarian has a relationship, and finally walk to a neighborhood grocery store in their "I'm Going to Kindergarten" T-shirts to pick up a free popsicle. If the librarians are hesitant about walking to a neighborhood vendor, they bring in pizza, cake, fruit, or vegetables.

Some of the best Kindergarten Day celebrations involved the local schools' principals or teachers, nonprofit organizations that offer health-care screenings or important safety information to parents, and obstacle courses (set up by children's librarians or local organizations). For last year's craft, the children made foam pennants stuck onto rulers with stickers and the name of their new school. Don't forget to have a special treat (such as pencil toppers or fun erasers) for the children who sign up for library cards at the celebration!

The Countdown team believes that project's strong success is due to continued collaboration among public, private, and nonprofit organizations throughout the city. Countdown to Kindergarten continues to grow locally and has expanded nationally to children's museums, libraries, and school systems.

About the Authors

Jeri Robinson is vice president of family learning and early childhood programs at Boston's Children's Museum and has taught and consulted in early childhood education for thirty-five years. She developed the PlaySpace exhibit (a prototype for museum early-learning family spaces), founded the Boston Cultural Collaborative for Early Learning, and cofounded Families First Parenting and Countdown to Kindergarten. Jeri received her BS, M.S.Ed., and an honorary doctorate in education from Wheelock College. In 2005, she was named to the American Association of Museums' Centennial Honor Roll in recognition of her contributions to the museum field. Jeri can be reached at robinson@ bostonchildrensmuseum.org.

Krystal Beaulieu is a program coordinator for Countdown to Kindergarten in Boston. She came to the program in 2006 after working on local policy reform with Governor Michael Dukakis. She earned her bachelor's degree in political science and journalism from Northeastern University. Krystal lives in the Savin Hill neighborhood of Boston with her fiancé and shih tzu puppy, Teddy Roosevelt. Krystal can be contacted at kbeaulieu@boston.k12.ma.us.

14

Saving Money through Family Literacy Collaborations

Wendy Blackwell, Leslie Gelders, Pam Cote, and Kerri McLinn

In August 2008, staff from the National Children's Museum (NCM) in Washington, D.C., traveled to Oklahoma to present a workshop, Family Literacy Projects on a Budget, to eight Ready to Learn trainers and several literacy staff from the Office of Literacy Resources in the Oklahoma Department of Libraries (ODL). The workshop was based on a simple and easy-to-use book for community educators offering resources, ideas, and helpful hints about ways to use low-cost and recycled items to develop and present effective literacy programs and related activities based on broad themes. Because of interest in the topic and the credentials of the presenters, ODL invited children's librarians, teachers, and family literacy providers to participate. Although the workshop was initially limited to twenty-five participants, because of a high level of interest, the list of attendees expanded to fifty. The NCM staff showed how to create a multitude of crafts and story extensions using low-cost and free materials. Workshop participants were thrilled with the number of ideas that were shared and were interested and involved during the fast-paced, enjoyable workshop.

Thanks to the NCM, ODL's expenses were minimal. Participants who traveled from across the state received travel reimbursement, and ODL provided hotel costs for the presenters. Participants brought free and low-cost everyday items from a list provided ahead of time. They shared their raw materials with one another so everyone was able to make bags full of samples to take home and use in their local programs.

For almost three decades, the Office of Literacy Resources in the ODL literacy office has worked with volunteer literacy councils that help adults improve their reading skills. In recent years, the office has expanded its services to support family and emergent literacy. Ready to Learn (RTL) is a collaborative project of ODL, the Oklahoma Educational Television Authority, and the Oklahoma Department of Human Resources (DHS); its focus is on providing books, resources, and teaching materials to aid children at risk for low literacy.

The ODL's Ready to Learn (RTL) trainers present emergent literacy workshops throughout the state for staff of DHS-certified child-care centers. Each year, the RTL project offers a new early literacy topic with different materials, resources, and training. Along with receiving a wealth of ideas and information, child-care staff receive continuing education credits required for DHS certification. According to Leslie Gelders, ODL's administrator, library staff is always on the lookout for resources and partnerships that can advance the office's mission: "When our staff member told us about the National Children's Museum program, we immediately saw that it could help with our Ready to Learn project."

ABOUT THE BOOK

Family Literacy Projects on a Budget: A Trainer's Toolkit, written by Wendy C. Blackwell, Jennifer Neale, Deborah Mason, Tisha Thorne, and Skye Hallman, organizes programs into themes, allowing program leaders to introduce families to many different books. Community agencies, professionals, artists, and other local groups are highlighted as invaluable resources that can provide useful information, support, and content to enrich literacy themes. The tool kit emphasizes that community involvement may start with just a simple invitation, and the workshop gives concrete examples of different programs.

Each chapter describes a different theme highlighting several books, activities that families can do together, and ways to link to the community via Internet, field trips, public television programming, and inviting in the community. Specific and unusual community connections are included in each chapter. For instance, the alphabet chapter suggests inviting a local cook or chef to help prepare alphabet soup for families to share at the literacy event that features either just one letter or the entire alphabet. Some other tips include the following:

> **Back to School.** Inviting the cafeteria staff to teach parents about healthy bag lunches, after-school snacks, and the school's policy on peanuts. Inviting the school nurse or other health-care practitioner to demonstrate the proper size and positioning for kids' backpacks to avoid back injury.

Bedtime Stories. Studies indicate that young children and some older adults can sleep through the sound of smoke detectors. Invite the fire department to distribute smoke detectors and tell families about emergency escape plans and meeting places.

Growing Challenges. This chapter featuring books about losing a pet, losing a tooth, wearing glasses, school, and friendship provides a great reason to have an intergenerational community party at which community members share their stories and make books together.

Illustration Replication. Because most children's books are beautifully illustrated using imaginative and creative techniques, this chapter encourages families to make books in the style of an illustrator using media like watercolors, torn paper, and etching. Community artists can be invited to share their creative ways to tell a story. A griot will use his voice; a dancer, her body; a musician will play an instrument; and a painter will use a brush.

Just the Facts and Who's Who. These activities highlight nonfiction books and introduce families to unusual professions like the piñata maker or the pea-shooting timekeeper. When a community explores these books together, families will meet inventors, magicians, realtors, upholsterers, veterinarians, and others. These meetings introduce children to careers and professions that they may not yet have encountered.

Not Your Inside Voice. This chapter celebrates advocates for the loud and rambunctious joy of boys featuring books like *I Stink*, by Kate and Jim McMullan (HarperCollins, 2002); *Dog Breath*, by Dav Pilkey (Blue Sky Press, 1994); *Walter the Farting Dog*, by William Kotzwinkle and Glenn Murray (Frog, 2001); and *Stanley Goes Ape*, by Griff (Hyperion, 2001). Family events feature careers and professions related to working outside, physical work that intrigues growing children and their parents like mounted police, garbage-truck drivers, band leaders, animal tamers, and zoo workers.

ABOUT THE COLLABORATION

Following the NCM training, ODL Ready to Learn trainers customized the information for the 2008–2009 workshop Make It, Take It, Teach It, which was offered to Oklahoma child-care providers. Each of thirty-two local workshops presented during the year incorporated books and craft suggestions acquired from the NCM training. Because Ready to Learn training promotes the use of the learning triangle—read, view, and do—trainers incorporated programs readily available on public television to coordinate with the theme and books selected. Each of the Ready to Learn trainers presented several local workshops across the state to share information with child-care providers and to demonstrate how storytimes could be enhanced through the use of free and low-cost craft activities. In addition, each child-care center received copies of the corresponding books and the NCM publication.

FAMILY LITERACY PROJECTS ON A BUDGET

Leslie Gelders said that feedback from the trainers and more than six hundred child-care providers was overwhelmingly positive: "Ready to Learn trainers are already planning how they will incorporate NCM information and resources in new training being developed for 2009–2010." The new workshop's theme is "Early Literacy through Science and Play." "The resources offered by the National Children's Museum are so good that every library, childcare center, and literacy program should have no problem adapting the examples to help their young children," according to ODL's Ready to Learn coordinator, Kerri McLinn. "These resources build literacy skills and help develop a lifetime love of reading," McLinn said, "and that's what our mission is all about."

OTHER COLLABORATIONS

The Sanford Community Adult Education Program in Maine crafted a different relationship with NCM. Pam Cote is the family literacy coordinator of Sanford Community Adult Education, part of Sanford Public Schools. With NCM, she created Families READ (Reach, Explore, Achieve, Dream), a Maine Family Literacy Lighthouse Project, funded by the Barbara Bush Foundation for Family Literacy. The Families READ program provides parents access to educational services to improve their skills as family members, workers, and community members. In its work with families, the program pursues four major goals:

1. To help parents improve their literacy skills needed to increase job opportunities

2. To help children reach their full potential as learners by the time they start school or as they continue through school

3. To help parents develop skills needed to teach, support, and advocate for their children

4. To help parents identify opportunities to learn and grow together.

Cote attended the National Children Museum's workshop Family Literacy Activities on a Budget at the National Center for Family Literacy's 2009 conference in Orlando, Florida. Impressed by Wendy Blackwell, her team, and their work, Pam contacted Wendy on her return to discuss a potential collaboration.

As chair of the conference Literacy Connections within Your Community in March 2009, Pam wanted to find a way to share the information she had received at the NCM workshop. She called Blackwell before the conference to discuss how they could work together to provide this information to Maine literacy providers. Wendy and her team put together chapter excerpts from their trainer's tool kit and created illustrative activities from their books for a display table. Because of this, Pam was able to discuss Family Projects on a Budget and provide an example of how collaborations can be made outside of one's immediate community. As a result of the information sharing, 235 conference participants were able to learn about the NCM and its resource book. In addition, each table's centerpiece was a hardcover book with an accompanying chapter excerpt. These were raffled off to participants at the end of the day. Clearly, Wendy Blackwell and the National Children's Museum staff believe in partnerships, and their willingness to collaborate helped to make Pam's conference successful.

In addition, the family literacy coordinator presented this topic at the June 2009 Maine Adult Education Association Conference, providing an opportunity for Pam to share the trainer's tool kit with adult educators, family literacy providers, early literacy providers, libraries, and other programs. This collaboration between Families READ and the National Children's Museum has become a true partnership. It is an example of programs working together to bring significant change to children and families.

By July 2009, the National Children's Museum had visited ten cities and developed collaborations with libraries in Minnesota and Maryland, where community educators use Family Projects on a Budget to implement family literacy programs. Other partners include the Prince George's County (Maryland) Early Childhood Interagency and CentroNía in Washington, D.C.

About the Authors

Wendy Camilla Blackwell, director of education for the National Children's Museum, is overseeing the development of education initiatives and the NCM Center for Learning and Innovation. Wendy believes that the excitement created by a good book can linger on forever and has set out to create memorable experiences for children and families with books, arts, and crafts. A mother of two and a textile artist, Wendy is also a former teacher who enjoys the education intersection where museum, library, school, community, children and families meet. She can be reached at wblackwell@ncm.museum.

Pam Cote is family literacy coordinator for Sanford Community Adult Education. Families READ recently won the Maine Family Literacy Lighthouse Project Grant from the Barbara Bush Foundation for Family Literacy for the second year. Pam currently teaches English classes and taught for several years at the elementary level. She previously was manager for Manpower Temporary Services, where she championed staff development and managed business relations with many of the firm's largest clients. Pam is active on several committees dedicated to the promotion of family literacy and school readiness in the Sanford and Springvale area. Pam can be contacted at pamcote@ sanford.org.

Leslie Gelders brings more than twenty-one years of adult literacy experience to the Oklahoma Department of Libraries' Literacy Resource Office. Her expertise as a tutor, trainer, grant writer, program developer, public speaker, and administrator has benefited libraries and literacy programs throughout Oklahoma. Although Leslie has shared her expertise on numerous state and national task forces and committees, her passion is helping local literacy programs provide quality services to their communities. She can be contacted at lgenders@oltn.odl.state.ok.us.

Kerri McLinn serves as the Ready to Learn coordinator for the Oklahoma Literacy Resource Office. Under her direction, new books are provided each month to more than 1,500 preschool children at risk for low literacy. Kerri coordinates emergent literacy workshops presented free of charge to child-care staff, teachers, and parents throughout the state. In addition, Kerri works with partner organizations to plan and present Read across Oklahoma, an annual literacy celebration attended by more than 1,500 children and 150 volunteers each April. She can be contacted at kmclinn@oltn.odl.state.ok.us.

four

Cultural Institutions
and Public Libraries

15

Small Libraries Help One Another in a Big Way

Leah Wagner

Middlesex County in New Jersey has a population of approximately 790,000. It is home to twenty-five libraries, the smallest serving a population of approximately 3,200 and the largest serving a population of approximately 97,500. The difference in library sizes and budgets creates limitations for the smaller libraries in the county. The professional organization Libraries of Middlesex (LMx) was created to provide opportunities for the municipal libraries in the county to work together and advocate for library service in the county. The majority of the libraries in LMx have only one or two youth services librarians, which makes it difficult for them to provide services or programs requiring more than one person. The LMx organization provides the opportunity for member libraries to benefit from the experience of the other libraries in LMx, as well as an opportunity for joint projects between and among the member libraries. The Children's Services Committee of LMx meets regularly in different county libraries to discuss upcoming projects and issues in youth services. This chapter discusses some of the programs made possible in small township libraries by LMx and its constituent libraries.

Summer reading is a primary focus of youth services in public libraries, and librarians are always seeking new and exciting ways to promote the current year's program and all the accompanying activities. For the smaller libraries staffed with only one children's librarian, LMx provided opportunities to reach a large number of children at once by conducting an assembly at the schools in the participating library's district. This program was completed on a very limited budget. Together, three librarians from different libraries met and created a script for a skit that incorporated the summer reading theme. The short skit features a gorilla who is encouraged to visit the local library, register for the summer reading program, and participate in the programs hosted by the local library. The gorilla not only discovers great books and a love of reading at the library but also has the opportunity to win prizes throughout the summer just for reading.

The skit was a joint activity, with each librarian adding specific information that pertained to his or her individual library, like the prizes being given away and additional programs that the library wanted to advertise. The script included humorous lines to grab young people's attention and many references to the local public library. The skit lasted approximately fifteen to twenty minutes and was offered to students in kindergarten through sixth grade. The skit could be performed on stage in the school auditorium or in a small area in the school media center. It was important to be flexible because each school visit was unique in its venue and in its audience. The goal was to engage young people and encourage them to visit their local library that summer.

The participating librarians scheduled the dates and times for the assembly with each school district. Each librarian was assigned a part in the skit and was responsible for creating the costume and collecting any necessary props. One year, the summer reading program included an original song that was included in the skit and proved a very successful addition. Promotional materials were not distributed, but this is something that could be considered to reinforce the library's message.

Puppet shows are a favorite among young children. Planning, rehearsing, and presenting them are time consuming and difficult for a library with a small staff. Through LMx, member libraries could borrow complete puppet-show favorites such as "Cinderella" and "Jack and the Beanstalk" that were designed, written, and created by a committee of LMx librarians. The committee, using resources found in the library, wrote the scripts. The committee either crafted the puppets for the show or purchased premade puppets. Scenes were created, props were collected, and music was recorded for use between scene changes. After several rehearsal sessions, each puppet show was presented at the participant's individual libraries to an excited and appreciative audience.

Working alone in a small library did not offer many occasions to discuss new and noteworthy titles in children's literature. The LMx committee chair created such an opportunity by arranging for book discussions to become part of regular committee meetings. Before each meeting, the group would hold a thirty- to forty-five-minute book discussion for the librarians. Depending on interest and available time, librarians could attend all of the discussions or just the ones in which they were interested. All attendees were required to read the selected title, and the committee chair ran the discussion. This proved an excellent opportunity for all the participants to work with the literature they were recommending to their own young library users.

Another major LMx activity is the creation of thematic and graded booklists. Again, this is particularly helpful for the professional in a smaller library without the staff to collect, edit, format, and print the list. The booklist committee collects titles from the youth services librarians and the subcommittee formats and edits the list. Once printed, each library receives a set number of booklists and a master to make additional copies if needed. As an outgrowth of this, another project was undertaken and a list of one hundred recommended books to read in kindergarten was created and distributed at the local library or to the local schools, depending on the library's preference. This list is in the form of a full-color poster and is costly to print. With the economy of scale created by the large number of libraries participating, printing becomes more reasonable and smaller libraries are able to purchase additional posters and provide a service that would be impossible without LMx.

Working with LMx allows the libraries to share many ideas. The group meets regularly and ends each meeting with presentations from the attending librarians describing their recent programs. Comments range from reports on programs or services that have proved successful or not, reviews of performers, and sometimes controversial or hot topics in youth services. The sessions have been very useful to the librarians who attend; many programs and services now provided in the member libraries have been created because of an idea suggested at an LMx meeting.

About the Author

Leah Wagner is the assistant director and youth services coordinator at the Monroe Township Public Library in New Jersey. She formerly was the children's librarian at the South River Public Library. She received her MLS from the Rutgers University School of Information and Library Science and her BS in elementary education from Trenton State College. Leah has served on numerous committees for the New Jersey Library Association, the Public Library Association's Services to Youth and their Parents Committee, and the New Jersey State Library's Children's Guidelines Committee. Leah can be contacted at lwagner@monroetwplibrary.org.

SmartArt

Ellen Riordan and Emily Blumenthal

The Enoch Pratt Free Library and the Walters Art Museum (WAM) are both cultural institutions with similar histories and missions. Only a block away from each other, in the Mount Vernon neighborhood of Baltimore, the two institutions had previously made use of each other's resources but had not collaborated in a meaningful and mutually beneficial way.

The Enoch Pratt Free Library, the nation's first free public library system, consists of a central library, an anchor library, twenty branches, two bookmobiles, a jail library, a technology-training center, and a regional information center. The Pratt's mission is "to provide equal access to information and services that support, empower, and enrich all who pursue knowledge, education, cultural enrichment, and lifelong learning" (www.prattlibrary.org/about/index.aspx?id=1826).

The Walters Art Museum's collection consists of almost thirty thousand works of art from around the world, from ancient Egypt to twentieth-century Europe and America. In October 2006, the WAM eliminated admission fees to make its collection more accessible to the public. After the first year, the WAM reported a 55 percent increase in attendance and a greater diversity in admissions. In fiscal year 2008, attendance was 203,497.

The mission of WAM is "to bring art and people together for enjoyment, discovery, and learning. We strive to create a place where people of every background can be touched by art. We are committed to exhibitions and programs that will strengthen and sustain our community" (http://thewalters.org/museum_art_baltimore/themuseum_mission.aspx).

Until 2001, collaboration between WAM and the Pratt was limited to museum docents occasionally borrowing books from the Pratt for WAM

programs. Staff educators from both institutions sustained professional relationships over the years, in part by participating in each other's signature
festival events. This entailed representatives from both institutions presenting
a preplanned activity to an event hosted by one of them. The activities were
not always related to the event directly and were viewed as an opportunity to
promote the programs and services of the institution but did not support a
shared vision or mission.

The WAM established its Department of Children and Family Programs in
2001, identifying family audiences and family-friendly programming as an institutional priority. With this transition came strategically planned programming,
interpretation of art, and strategic partnerships to best serve Baltimore's community. At the Pratt, programs for children and families were being revamped
to include consistent, well-planned library experiences for children under the
age of five. Emerging studies indicated that those years were critical ones for
enabling children to realize their optimum potential later in life.

As their respective institutions expanded their work with families and young
children, the newly formed Department of Children and Family Programs
of WAM and Pratt's burgeoning Office of Children's Services met to discuss
joint initiatives and created interpretive gallery kiosks, called ArtCarts, with the
intention of integrating children's literature and bridging the central library
and WAM. ArtCarts represented the transition of the relationship from one
of reaching out to one of shared projects. The project was challenged by the
absence of a common goal and was ultimately not successful.

In 2003, the Pratt was asked to participate in a leadership development program funded by a local nonprofit with national mission and focus. The purpose
of this program was to rally leaders from like-minded city agencies and nonprof-
its toward a common goal of improving school readiness of Baltimore's children
by November 2004. The term *school readiness* refers to the point at which a
young child reaches established standards of emotional, social, physical, and
cognitive benchmarks to enable him or her to succeed in the structured world
of a kindergarten classroom. The indicators for assessing these goals were well
established through the Maryland Model of School Readiness and the testing
device known as the Work Sampling System.

In September 2004, to raise awareness about the importance of school
readiness and to get information immediately into the hands of parents and
caregivers of young children, a public engagement campaign that focused on
the citywide efforts of school readiness was formed. Countdown to Kindergarten Baltimore aligned with the statewide school-readiness efforts of the same
name already taking place at the state level. As a result of the public awareness
campaign, the Pratt became a member of a subcommittee whose purpose was
to identify cultural partners in the city that were interested in aligning their
outreach programming to focus on young children and their families under
the umbrella of broad programming in service to Countdown to Kindergarten.

Because the coordinator of children's services of the Pratt, Ellen Riordan, had worked with the staff of WAM in the past through program sharing and the ArtCarts project, she seized on this new impetus to strengthen the partnership between them. She invited her contact at WAM, Emily Blumenthal, to attend a meeting of the Countdown to Kindergarten Family and Community Engagement Committee. From this meeting, WAM was able to align its work with a larger citywide mission that was having a measurable effect on Baltimore's children. The Pratt and WAM have been active members of the Family and Community Engagement Committee of Countdown to Kindergarten since 2005.

With a well-established partnership and shared committee responsibilities that contributed to a citywide initiative, both institutions decided to move the relationship forward by planning and implementing a program together. Both WAM and the Pratt already offered activities designed for the youngest customers at their large family events. These early childhood programs required unique planning and staffing. The program area required interactive experiences and needed to be designed to encourage adult caregivers and young children to engage in some activities together. With these factors in mind, a team from WAM and the Pratt met together to plan an early childhood activity together that could be used at major family events in both institutions. They called the project SmartArt, because it brings together art and literacy in ways that expand education opportunities for Baltimore's young children.

PROGRAM DETAILS

Objective

The objective of this project was to create an early childhood area for children from birth to the age of five and their families as a critical element of two major family events using the shared expertise of the collaborative entities.

Program Title

Play with the Frog Prince Early Childhood Area

Program Description

The Walters Art Museum and the Enoch Pratt Free Library created together an early childhood area, Play with The Frog Prince, which functioned as a literacy and sensory experience for young children. The area took the story "The Frog Prince" and broke down the elements of the narrative into a series of six age-appropriate activities. The library staff worked with the museum to brainstorm the various areas of the narrative: the princess drops her ball, the frog follows her to dinner, she kisses him, and the frog transforms. The museum helped render these narrative elements into activities. Signage provided simple text that helped focus the young children and their caregivers, move them through the exhibit, and emphasize targeted development domains. The children hopped like a frog on a path of lily pads from one area to the next. "The princess played with her gold ball. Roll the ball to the fountain," was the sign placed by a wading pool with plastic balls that could be rolled and counted and moved from one place to another. "The princess and the frog eat dinner together. Make dinner for the frog and the princess" was placed by a child-sized table with plates, spoons, and cups. Soft frogs could be placed on and off the table to help act out the scene. Children "kissed" the frog by stamping lips on a large picture of a frog. Nearby, a mirror along with masks that had frog princes on one side and princes and princesses on the other made the transformation complete. Finally, children and their caregivers were able to read "The Frog Prince" together, enjoying various versions of the story and other fairy tales.

Program Location, Dates, and Audience Statistics

Event: Fairy Tale Festival
Location: Enoch Pratt Free Library, Central Library
Date and Time: April 4, 2009, 10 a.m.–3 p.m., and April 5, 2009,
    1 p.m.–3 p.m.
Age and Audience: 0–5 (49 percent), 6–12 (3 percent), and adults
    (48 percent)
Total Attendance: 605

Event: Once upon a Time Family Festival
Location: Walters Art Museum
Date and Time: April 25, 2009, 10 a.m.–4 p.m.
Age and Audience: All ages, primarily 0–5 and adults
Total Attendance: 883

Publicity

Each institution publicized its event separately, highlighting the partner institution and the creation of a separate early childhood area. Promotional efforts included the Pratt's *Fairy Tale Gazette*, WAM's Family Fun Spring 2009 postcard, e-newsletters and e-blasts, features on the institutions' websites, and social media postings, among others. In addition, each institution cross-promoted both events.

Staff and Equipment Needs

Staff from the Pratt and WAM conducted program planning meetings and ongoing communication regarding the project. Meetings were scheduled in August 2008 (initial collaborative project agreement, scheduling, and brainstorm session) and in January 2009 (fleshing out of the idea, writing of the narrative elements, and dividing responsibilities). Throughout the entire process, staff members from each institution communicated through e-mail to follow up on and define project details.

To plan and conduct the events, each institution required two staff members, for a total of four. The project necessitated that the staff invest in planning and production hours. The Pratt contributed eight to ten planning hours; the WAM contributed ten to twelve planning hours and fifteen to twenty production hours, in addition to the unique expertise that its staff members contributed. During the working process, the library staff took the lead on the narrative and literary components, and the museum staff led interactive and rendering components. Furthermore, the two institutions shared many in-house resources to produce the early childhood area without an additional program budget. The total cost, which the Pratt and WAM shared, was $518, and the list of supplies is as follows:

Stamping kisses on the frog . . . Will he turn into a prince?

Supply List

Description	Quantity	Description	Quantity
Activity sheet	300	Mirror	1
Beanbags and pillows	assorted	Plastic play dinner set	1
Books	6	Rug	1
Castle	1	Signage	10
Colored pencils	assorted	Stamps	5
Easels	2	Table and chairs set	1
Foam kiddy pool	1	Tables	1
Frog prints	3	Toy frogs	4
Frog and prince masks	6	Velcro	1 box
Gold toy balls	6	Washable ink pads	4
Hand wipes	4 tubs	Education assistant staff	2 people on
Laminating sleeves	1 box		3 event dates
Lily pads	20		

With the expansion of collaborative efforts between the Pratt and WAM, and the ensuing efforts enabling both institutions to join forces with others to further a civic goal, both institutions came to value the strengths of the other and the opportunities for cross-promotion and collaboration of programming. The result is mutual realization of their mission statements. Currently, the staffs of WAM and the Pratt are planning new ways to work together.

About the Authors

Ellen Riordan is coordinator of children's services for Baltimore's Enoch Pratt Free Library. Under her management, the library instituted the Fairy Tale Festival and the First Card program. She participates in the Reach Out and Read Advisory Committee, the Baltimore Leadership in Action program, and the Capitol Choices book-evaluation group. A board member of the Association of Library Services to Children, in 2006 she was elected American Library Association councilor for 2006–2009. Her article "Make Way for Dendrites" appeared in the Spring 2004 issue of *Children and Libraries*. She is mother to Daniel and Lillian. Contact her at eriordan@epfl.net.

Emily Blumenthal is manager of children and family programs at Baltimore's Walters Art Museum, where she develops and implements materials and programs to engage families and children with works of art. Emily is a member of the Parent and Community Engagement Committee of Countdown to Kindergarten and has frequently presented research on family programs and museum learning. For the past four years, she has been a mentor for the Maryland Institute College of Art's exhibition development seminar. Emily received her MS in leadership in museum education from the Bank Street Graduate College of Education. Contact her at eblumenthal@thewalters.org.

Teaching Storytelling to Youth

A Library, a School, and an Art Institute Collaborate

Cathy Lancaster and Brenda Harris

Flint Public Library (FPL) is located in Michigan's Flint Cultural Center (FCC), which comprises a music institute and an art institute, multiple theaters, museums, and a planetarium. The Pierce-Sarvis Branch of Pierce Elementary houses fifth and sixth graders and is located in the Flint Community School's Sarvis Center, on the FCC campus. Pierce-Sarvis developed a regular routine for students to walk over to the library, receive regular lessons in library skills, check out books, and use library resources.

Brenda Harris, a storyteller and library assistant (currently working toward her MLIS) was introduced to techniques for using storytelling with elementary students at a storytelling conference. In an effort to expand the interaction between librarians and students, *Children Tell Stories: Teaching and Using Storytelling in the Classroom* by Martha Hamilton and Mitch Weiss (2005) was purchased and a storytelling course shaped by this text was developed for the Pierce-Sarvis sixth graders. The resulting collaborative effort between FPL's children's room staff, Pierce-Sarvis teachers, and the educational coordinator of the Flint Institute of Arts used a storytelling unit as a unique opportunity to work on literary skills (writing and reading), performance skills (presenting stories), and artistic skills (illustrating written stories) with sixth graders. Students heard and studied folklore and fables, wrote their own version of a folktale, learned to perform their tale, and had the chance to illustrate their tales.

THE PROCESS

Each Pierce-Sarvis sixth-grade class has approximately twenty-five ten- to twelve-year-olds. From September through May, a monthly library visit is scheduled for each class, during which students work on their storytelling projects and have a chance to browse the children's room collection. They work in small groups, coaching one another, and by the end of the session, each student presents a story to the class. After the visit, the teacher continues the exercise in class and sends the results to the library via e-mail attachment. A booklet of the final short stories is compiled for all participants.

The students start with a simple assignment: write an alliteration tale, in which every word begins with the same letter, in five or fewer sentences. (This assignment was borrowed from *Children Tell Stories*.)

The visit after alliterations introduces Aesop's fables. Then each child is given a story kernel: a basic plot and characters. Working in groups, the children help one another create an entire story. They complete a visualization chart in which they are asked to describe their characters and the setting in detail. The students then fill in a character analysis chart to help develop their characters for performance. Finally, they create a storyboard of the entire tale to draw out the plot. This process enables the students to write their entire unique fable and revise it in several drafts in class under teacher supervision.

On subsequent visits, performing techniques are discussed and demonstrated. Both the best and worst ways to communicate tales to an audience are exemplified. Eye contact, gestures, and voicing are practiced using a variety of performance techniques while presenting short poems and nursery rhymes. Several theater exercises build comfort and skill levels in presenting to an audience. Students present the final draft of their tale in a storytelling session at

Pierce-Sarvis students begin their projects with a visit to the Flint Public Library.

VISUALIZATION

Create a moving picture of the story in your mind and convey the pictures to listeners.

Use voice and action to convey setting (location, place, and time), character(s), and events.

See actions, share feelings, and know the mood of the story.

Get in touch with *your* senses and convey a story through your senses.

EXERCISES: Use senses to describe a scene: sight, hearing, smell, taste, touch, and emotions.

- Using only one sense, describe a place, an event, a person, or an object to a partner.
- Describe your favorite place using sensory words. Ask for a listener's response.
- Below list sensory words for each sense. Write a sentence using these words.

SENSES	WORD LIST	WRITE *ONE* SENTENCE
Sight		
Hearing		
Smell		
Taste		
Touch		
Emotions		

CHARACTER ANALYSIS

Describe your characters:

1. Name the character and list its identifying quality, or physical trait.
2. Complete the chart sections for each character. Be very descriptive, add details, use all your senses.
3. Keep these details in mind as you write your story.

Mental description: What does the character think about?	Emotional description: How does the character feel?	Physical descriptions: What does character look like?	Age & Relationship to other characters	Character Name & Identifier	Primary or other?

STORY BOARD

Use this **STORY BOARD** to describe the plot steps in your story. Use as many sheets as needed.
Draw a simple picture that describes the action and write a sentence about the action below your picture.

TITLE	OPENING LINES	
AUTHOR		
1	2	3
Sentence	Sentence	Sentence
4	5	6
Sentence	Sentence	Sentence
REPEATING LINES	THINGS TO REMEMBER	CLOSING LINES

109

the library. At this stage, students can still use note cards or papers as backup while presenting.

The last section focuses on creating *pourquoi* tales, stories or folktales that explain how or why something exists, usually in the natural world. The Pierce-Sarvis teachers will have already introduced these tales to their students. The librarian shares several *pourquoi* tales and discusses how they were used to explain the unexplainable in a community's life. A story kernel from which the student can build a story is offered, or children can invent a new tale from their own imagination. Although some students find creative writing difficult, the story kernel helps by offering a basic story line, characters, and setting details on which students can build their unique version of the tale. After listening to different versions of the same tale (for example, the variations of "Cinderella," "The Three Pigs," or "Jack and the Beanstalk"), students are encouraged to embellish the kernel and create a personal version of their story. Discussions center on the viewpoint from which the story is being told and the character telling the story. By this time, the students feel confident in writing their own fable and many invent their own tales.

The teachers take charge of much of the writing and rehearsals with the students, because class visits to the library are limited. Teachers ensure that the writing is edited and completed, that storytelling practicing is done, and that students are selected for a final presentation. The polished tales are presented in a storytelling session at the library. The teachers may arrange to have their students present their tales in groups to children in the lower elementary grades. Students may also be given the opportunity to present their stories to senior citizens or other community groups; however, this requires support from both the school and parents. The students embrace this process of writing and performing.

In addition to writing and performing their tales, Pierce-Sarvis sixth graders also created vivid illustrations for their writing through the collaboration with the Flint Institute of Art, under the guidance of Janet Friesen, the educational coordinator. Using art to emphasize the storytelling unit, Friesen found, "The students were eager to learn printmaking, collage, and painting so they could adapt these techniques to their illustrations. Students were motivated to 'get to work' on their art and did not hesitate to apply their skills with confidence. They came to class with thumbnail sketches and plans, which were used to create story illustrations. Students demonstrated a level of personal involvement in making art due to immersion in the subject and the process of learning." Their art included visual images, colors, shapes, and details that complemented their language arts learning. A library assistant built a website featuring the tales and their illustrations. Friesen photographed the students' work for the website and hung the exhibit in the library for public viewing.

Students selected representatives from each class to be part of a year-end performance. The teachers related that, although there "was no formal evaluation . . . students showed enthusiasm for the interdisciplinary project and demonstrated good writing skills. They appeared to be proud of their writing, their artwork and their storytelling. It gave them an opportunity to present their work to the community."

Students and families have visited the website (www.fpl.info/kidsweb/Pierce Sarvis/index.shtml). The students' last names are shielded for their privacy protection on both the website and in the art exhibit. For the 2010 collaboration, a teacher plans to record snippets of their tales as an added feature to be

Student artwork illustrates their original stories.

streamed on the website. In 2009, the public library plans to publish a small book containing all the unique stories with the students' illustrations bound and placed in the library's collection.

CONSIDERATIONS

Storytelling is a fun way to approach several practical skills that students need to develop while also exploring folklore and fables and seeing the world though the experiences and stories of others. This unit allows students to approach writing constructively and creatively. In 2008, the first show-and-tell was hosted at FPL, where the selected students presented their stories with a slide show of all student artwork running behind them on stage. This was followed by a small reception in the children's room, where families, teachers, and school administrators browsed the art on display. The 2009 performance became a preview show for the students' theater performances at the Flint Youth Theatre, another branch of the Pierce-Sarvis collaborative with the Flint Cultural Center. A slide show of the art ran above the stage before the show began. Friesen, from the Flint Institute of Arts, narrated how "prior to the art lessons the students had already thought through their ideas for their art work through preliminary writing, discussion, and reading" of the stories. A group of students performed their stories in a small studio near the main theater about thirty minutes before the show. Afterward, students, families, and school staff

Students express original stories through dance.

walked next door to a reception at the library, where the original artwork was on display for the month.

DOS AND DON'TS

Students may choose whether to receive constructive criticism from their peers, their teachers, and the librarian. All criticism must be respectful, encouraging, and limited to three or four comments per story to keep things going. Students are asked to begin all feedback with one of these phrases: "I wonder if" or "I like that." "I wonder if" is a chance to make suggestions, and "I like that" begins a sentence that compliments the person's efforts. This technique is borrowed from Karen Chace's "Story by Story" presentation at the 2007 National Storytelling Conference, which taught the skill of making gentle, respectful, constructive criticism through the process of learning how to tell stories.

THE COLLABORATION

All three institutions in this collaboration worked both independently throughout the process and closely together for the end result. E-mail kept communication between organizations and staff open and current. Librarians took turns working with the students; each librarian was proficient in an area so that none of the duties fell on one person. Everyone worked together to create a memorable experience for the children.

Friesen found the collaborative "an excellent example of a comprehensive art lesson that combines visual arts learning with core curriculum subjects." One goal of the Flint Institute of Arts was to design art lessons that brought learning to life with exciting art experiences to enhance classroom learning, and this collaborative experience was a perfect example of that process. "One important advantage of collaboration between schools and cultural institutions," Friesen continued, was "that it opens up the doors of the classroom to access learning resources in the wider community. The art museum, the public library, the theater, and the schools were partners in teaching children as a unified effort to create meaningful learning." The teacher Sue Sumner, from Pierce-Sarvis, found that "the collaborative provides the classroom teachers a partnership with experts in the field of art and storytelling. It draws upon the talents of these experts which the classroom teachers incorporate into the students' everyday learning experience."

Collaboration costs were relatively low, as they relied on library and school resources. A small budget covered art supplies, printing costs, and treats. Equipment included an LCD projector and screen and a word processor for handouts and materials. The bimonthly library calendar and postcards sent home to parents and school administration provided publicity for the show-and-tell. In recognition, all students received an Applause Award, which came from Karen Chace's workshop and stands for

Audience: Make eye contact
Pacing: Not too fast, not too slow, just right
Pronunciation: Say your words clearly
Love your story
Avoid distractions
Use the right tone of voice for your characters
Smile
Expression

Resources

Chace, Karen. "Story by Story: Building a School Storytelling Club Workshop." Presented at the National Storytelling Conference, July 2007. www.storytellingwithchildren.com/2008/05/12/karen-chace-school-storytelling-club/.

Hamilton, Martha, and Mitch Weiss. *Children Tell Stories: Teaching and Using Storytelling in the Classroom.* New York: Richard C. Owen, 2005.

Parent, Michael. "Grab the Space! Storytelling Basics Workshop." Presented at the National Storytelling Conference, July 2007.

Sima, Judy, and Kevin Cordi. *Raising Voices: Creating Youth Storytelling Groups and Troupes.* Westport, CT: Libraries Unlimited, 2003.

About the Authors

Catherine G. Lancaster, a children's librarian at Flint Public Library since 2003, has been on multiple committees and collaborated with the Flint Cultural Center on a variety of programs for children and families. In 2004, she developed the toddler storytime "Hear and Say," based on the six skills for early literacy presented by the Public Library Association. Cathy enjoys developing storytimes and programs for children. She can be reached at clancaster@fpl.info.

Brenda P. Harris has been assistant librarian for the Flint Public Library since 1992 and a storyteller in the Genesee County community for over twenty years. She believes that stories transmit a sense of the past, illuminate the present, and cultivate a vision for the future. Brenda presents traditional, historical and multicultural tales, programs, and workshops for children and adults. She is currently completing her MLIS at Wayne State University. Brenda can be reached at bharris@fpl.info.

five

Businesses and Public Libraries

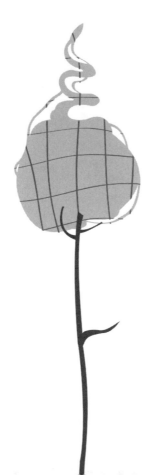

Science in the Summer©

Margie Stern

Science in the Summer is a free six-week program that engages children in standards-based science and mathematics activities at local public libraries. Rising second through sixth graders attend weeklong classes taught by certified teachers and explore bioscience, chemistry, oceanography, physical science, simple machines, or genetics. The objective of the Science in the Summer program, sponsored by GlaxoSmithKline, is to introduce science to young students and take advantage of the fact that they learn best by doing. This year, the program celebrates twenty-three years of instilling the excitement of science through hands-on experimentation.

On any given day during the summer in libraries throughout Philadelphia and the surrounding four-county region you may find children making compasses; learning how to use an electrostatic generator; making crystals and performing experiments with litmus paper to learn about acids, bases, and indicators; using microscopes, microviewers, and magnifying glasses to observe, touch, draw, and learn about sea creatures; observing a variety of cells and dissecting a flower to study its different parts; or learning how machines do amazing things such as lift huge boulders, build bridges, and pump water or how to extract DNA from a strawberry.

GlaxoSmithKline Science in the Summer was the vision of the scientist Dr. Virginia Cunningham. Cunningham, at the time, headed the SmithKline Beecham Environmental Research Laboratory. She saw a need to attract female and minority students to enter the field of science. Cunningham wanted the experience to be fun and not related to school. "Where do children go in the summer?" she asked at a social event that, coincidentally, both a librarian and a teacher attended. The public library was the immediate response of both.

So, in the late 1980s, partnering with a local teacher and the children's librarian at the Montgomery County Norristown Public Library, the development and implementation of a one-week summer science course was formulated. That first session for thirty children has evolved into a highly successful six-week program that serves about six thousand students annually at 143 libraries in the city of Philadelphia and surrounding four-county library systems. To date, about ninety-six thousand students have participated.

The Free Library of Philadelphia, Bucks County Public Libraries, Chester County Library System, Delaware County Library System, and the Montgomery County Library District all receive grant funds directly from Glaxo-

Goggled campers listen with rapt attention.

SmithKline. Each county uses the funds to pay the salaries of the teachers, to purchase equipment and supplies needed for each particular course, and to buy high-quality science-related books to support the various courses. Further collaboration includes sharing the larger, more expensive equipment such as microscopes, electrostatic generators, superconductor levitation kits, and magnetic field observation boxes. Equipment is rotated from county to county each year.

The success of Science in the Summer is due to the collaborative efforts between the committed partners, each with its distinct strengths that help strengthen and expand the program. The partners include GlaxoSmithKline, a pharmaceutical company, the funder and a major employer in the target community; the American Association for the Advancement of Science (AAAS), the program administrator and nonprofit science organization with more than 150,000 members; the youth services coordinators of the five library districts (Bucks, Chester, Delaware, and Montgomery counties and the Free Library of Philadelphia); and highly qualified area K–12 teachers.

The multiyear relationship, as described previously, began on a small scale: one scientist, one teacher, and one county library system. It grew slowly, first within the library system, and then in 1993 it expanded to surrounding counties and the city of Philadelphia. The entire region encompasses urban, suburban, and rural areas, and each library has its unique strengths and concerns. The relationship over time has given the partners the opportunity to test and refine strategies needed to establish, maintain, and expand the collaboration.

The following practices have proved successful and can be emulated in other collaborative projects. First, it is important to keep in contact with all partners. With Science in the Summer, this occurs before, during, and after the program. Beginning in January and up to the start of the summer, meetings are held with the library coordinators, teachers, and local librarians. The meetings serve as a conduit for everyone to share information, give feedback, offer suggestions, share frustrations, and deal with problems.

Evaluation of the program has been an important component from the beginning. GlaxoSmithKline, AAAS, and library coordinators conduct regular site visits and observations while the program is in session. There is opportunity for all partners to provide written feedback through evaluations and reports. Updates to content materials and program structure are made on the basis of evaluation and feedback.

Finally, and most important, celebrate success. At the conclusion of the program, each summer partner attends a celebratory dinner to share highlights

A Science in the Summer participant proudly displays her circuit.

of the program and to award certificates of participation in a relaxed, informal setting.

For further information about Science in the Summer, visit www.sciencein thesummer.com.

About the Author

Margie Stern is the coordinator of youth services for Pennsylvania's Delaware County Library System. She previously worked in several local libraries as the children's librarian. She earned her MLS from Drexel University and BA from Slippery Rock University. Margie can be reached at mstern@delco libraries.org.

Index

You may also be interested in

The Early Literacy Kit: Ideal for program planners, this convenient resource will help you teach caregivers the developing standards by which school readiness can be achieved. The kit includes an accessible handbook with a resource section, 105 reusable tip cards with coordinated activities, and a concise summary of important early literacy research.

Booktalking Bonanza: Transform your booktalks to engage your audience! With multimedia infusing nearly every activity, today's audiences from toddlers to elders expect lively, interactive presentations. Get up to speed with exciting media technologies like YouTube videos, online music, PowerPoint presentations, Internet resources, and audio and video from the library collection, along with food, games, puppets, and magic or science experiments.

Twenty-First-Century Kids, Twenty-First-Century Librarians: This thoroughly researched book includes the current issues and trends of outcome-based planning, early literacy, homework centers, children's spaces, and much more. With extensive experience in children's services as well as library instruction issues, Walter brings readers vital information on the current state of library services to children.

From Children's Literature to Readers Theatre: Elizabeth A. Poe, creator of many Readers Theatre programs, explains how to create successful programs, offering ways you can link basic educational goals with appreciation of good literature, a bibliography of books suggested for their Readers Theatre potential, with examples of texts converted into scripts, and core programming ideas that can be adapted for use across different age levels.

Order today at www.alastore.ala.org or 866-746-7252!

ALA Store purchases fund advocacy, awareness, and accreditation programs for library professionals worldwide.

ORDER TODAY!

Mail in this order form or visit
WWW.ALASTORE.ALA.ORG

ALA Member #   (Must provide to receive your discount.)

☐ home   ☐ organization

E-MAIL ADDRESS (REQUIRED in case we have questions about your order.)

Daytime Phone

Ship to

NAME

TITLE

ORGANIZATION

ADDRESS

CITY   STATE   ZIP

METHOD OF PAYMENT

☐ Check or money order enclosed $_____
(Make payable to ALA)

☐ Bill my library, school or organization. (Only orders of $50 or more from established organizational accounts can be billed.)

☐ Purchase Order #_____ (Only for billed orders to libraries, schools or other organizations. First-time customers, please provide organizational purchase order.)

☐ VISA   ☐ MasterCard   ☐ American Express

☐☐☐☐ ☐☐☐☐ ☐☐☐☐ ☐☐☐☐
Credit Card Number

☐☐ / ☐☐
Exp. Date

SIGNATURE

FEDERAL TAX I.D. NUMBER

(Library, Bookstore)

ISBN	Title	qty.	unit price	10% Member discount*	total (qty. × unit price – discount)

METHOD OF SHIPPING

All orders are sent UPS Ground Service unless otherwise specified*. For the following alternate shipping options, call 1-866-SHOP ALA for a shipping quote.

☐ UPS 2nd Day Air (Cost plus $20)

☐ UPS Next Day Air (Cost plus $10)

*AK, HI, Puerto Rico, U.S. Virgin Islands, and Guam orders must select UPS 2nd Day.

SHIPPING & HANDLING CHARGES WILL BE ADDED TO ALL ORDERS

Within the U.S.:
Up to $49.99 . . . . $9
$50 to $99.99. . . . . $11
$100 to $149.99. . . . . $13
$150 to $199.99. . . . . $14
$200 to $299.99. . . . . $15
$300 to $999.99. . . . . $20
$1,000+ . . . . .Call 866-776-7252

For bulk rates, call 800-545-2433, ext. 2427

subtotal

sales tax **

shipping and handling (see chart above)

order total

*Member discounts do not apply to special offers or sets. **Discounts are not combined.**

**Residents of IL, CT, DC, or GA who are not tax exempt, please add appropriate sales tax. If you are unsure of your tax rate, call 1-866-746-7252 for assistance. If you are tax exempt, please include a copy of your tax-exempt certificate with your order.

IMPORTANT: Only orders of $50 or more from established organizational accounts can be billed.